PIE TOWN

Publications International, Ltd.

Front cover image: Shutterstock.com

Pictured on the back cover *(left to right):* Sweet Potato Pecan Pie *(page 66),* Shoofly Pie *(page 12)* and Speedy Double Strawberry Cream Pie *(page 136).*

ISBN: 978-1-68022-087-2

Library of Congress Control Number: 2015938821

Manufactured in China.

8 7 6 5 4 3 2 1

Microwave Cooking: Microwave ovens vary in wattage. Use the cooking times as guidelines and check for doneness before adding more time.

Publications International, Ltd.

Table of Contents

✶ All-American Classics ✶

Southern Oatmeal Pie

Makes
8 servings

1 refrigerated pie crust (half of 15-ounce package)

4 eggs

1 cup light corn syrup

½ cup packed brown sugar

6 tablespoons (¾ stick) butter, melted and cooled slightly

1½ teaspoons vanilla

½ teaspoon salt

1 cup quick oats

Whipped cream (optional)

1 Let crust stand at room temperature 15 minutes. Preheat oven to 375°F. Line 9-inch pie plate with crust; flute edge.

2 Beat eggs in medium bowl. Add corn syrup, brown sugar, butter, vanilla and salt; beat until well blended. Stir in oats. Pour into crust.

3 Bake 35 minutes or until edge is set. Cool on wire rack. Serve warm or at room temperature with whipped cream, if desired.

Peanut Chocolate Surprise Pie

Makes
8 servings

½ cup (1 stick) butter, melted and cooled slightly

1 cup sugar

2 eggs

½ cup all-purpose flour

½ cup chopped peanuts

½ cup chopped walnuts

½ cup semisweet chocolate chips

¼ cup bourbon

1 teaspoon vanilla

1 unbaked 9-inch deep-dish pie crust

Whipped cream (optional)

Chocolate curls (optional)

1 Preheat oven to 350°F.

2 Beat butter and sugar in large bowl with electric mixer at medium speed until creamy. Add eggs; beat until well blended. Gradually beat in flour at low speed just until blended. Stir in peanuts, walnuts, chocolate chips, bourbon and vanilla until blended. Spread evenly in unbaked crust.

3 Bake 40 minutes. Cool on wire rack. Top with whipped cream and chocolate curls, if desired.

Deep-Dish Country Apple Pie

Makes
8 servings

5 cups sliced peeled Gala apples

3 cups sliced peeled Granny Smith apples

1 tablespoon lemon juice

2 teaspoons vanilla

½ cup sugar

¼ cup all-purpose flour

½ teaspoon ground cinnamon

¼ teaspoon ground nutmeg

2 tablespoons butter, cut into small pieces

1 refrigerated pie crust (half of 15-ounce package)

1 Preheat oven to 425°F.

2 Combine apples, lemon juice and vanilla in large bowl; toss to coat. Add sugar, flour, cinnamon and nutmeg; toss again. Pour into 9-inch deep-dish pie plate; dot with butter.

3 Place crust over apples; flute edge, if desired. Cut several slits in crust with tip of knife.

4 Bake 50 minutes or until apples are tender. (Cover edge with foil during last 15 minutes if crust is browning too quickly.) Serve warm or at room temperature.

Old-Fashioned Coconut Meringue Pie

Makes
8 servings

1¼ cups sugar, divided

½ cup self-rising flour

1¼ cups milk

3 eggs, separated

1 teaspoon vanilla

2 tablespoons butter

1¼ cups flaked coconut, divided

1 baked 9-inch pie crust

1 Preheat oven to 350°F.

2 Combine 1 cup sugar and flour in medium saucepan. Beat in milk, egg yolks, vanilla and butter until well blended. Cook over medium heat until mixture thickens, whisking constantly. Remove from heat; stir in 1 cup coconut. Pour into baked crust.

3 Beat egg whites in medium bowl with electric mixer at high speed until foamy. Gradually add remaining ¼ cup sugar, beating until soft peaks form. Spread over filling, covering completely. Sprinkle with remaining ¼ cup coconut.

4 Bake 10 to 15 minutes or until meringue is golden brown. Cool on wire rack.

Shoofly Pie

Makes
8 servings

1 cup all-purpose flour

⅔ cup packed brown sugar

¼ cup (½ stick) plus 1 tablespoon butter, cut into small pieces, divided

3 eggs, beaten

½ cup molasses

½ teaspoon baking soda

⅔ cup hot water

1 unbaked 9-inch deep-dish pie crust

Whipped cream (optional)

1 Preheat oven to 325°F.

2 Combine flour and brown sugar in medium bowl. For topping, remove ½ cup flour mixture to small bowl. Cut in 1 tablespoon butter with pastry blender or two knives until mixture resembles coarse crumbs.

3 Melt remaining ¼ cup butter in small heavy saucepan over low heat; cool slightly. Beat eggs, molasses and melted butter in large bowl until blended. Gradually stir in flour mixture until well blended. Stir in baking soda. Gradually stir in water until blended. Pour into unbaked crust. Sprinkle with topping.

4 Bake 40 minutes or until filling is puffy and set. Cool completely on wire rack. Serve with whipped cream, if desired.

Lattice-Topped Cherry Pie

Makes
8 servings

Pie Pastry (recipe follows)

6 cups pitted sweet Bing cherries

¾ cup sugar, plus additional for top of pie

3 tablespoons plus 1 teaspoon cornstarch

2 tablespoons lemon juice

Half-and-half

1 Prepare Pie Pastry. Preheat oven to 400°F. Combine cherries, ¾ cup sugar, cornstarch and lemon juice in large bowl; toss to coat. Let stand 15 minutes or until syrup forms.

2 Roll out one disc of dough into 12- to 13-inch circle, about ⅛ to ¼ inch thick, between sheets of waxed paper. Line 9-inch pie plate with dough, allowing excess to drape over edge of pie plate. Roll out remaining disc of dough; cut into 12 to 14 strips about ½ inch wide.

3 Pour cherry filling into crust. Arrange strips in lattice design over filling. Tuck ends of strips under bottom crust; press to seal. Brush crust with half-and-half; sprinkle with additional sugar. Cover loosely with foil.

4 Bake 30 minutes. Remove foil; bake 30 minutes or until filling is thick and bubbly and crust is golden brown. Cool on wire rack.

Pie Pastry: Combine 2¼ cups all-purpose flour and ¾ teaspoon salt in medium bowl. Cut in ½ cup cold cubed shortening and 2 tablespoons cold cubed butter with pastry blender or two knives until mixture resembles coarse crumbs. Gradually add 5 tablespoons cold water; mix with fork until dough forms, adding additional water as needed. Divide dough in half. Shape each half into a disc; wrap with plastic wrap. Refrigerate 15 minutes.

Mixed Berry Skillet Pie

Makes
8 servings

2   packages (12 ounces each) frozen mixed berries

⅓   cup sugar

3   tablespoons cornstarch

2   teaspoons grated orange peel

¼   teaspoon ground ginger

1   refrigerated pie crust (half of 15-ounce package)

1   Preheat oven to 350°F.

2   Combine berries, sugar, cornstarch, orange peel and ginger in large bowl; toss to coat. Pour into large cast iron skillet.

3   Roll out pie crust into 12-inch circle. Place over fruit mixture in skillet; crimp edge as desired. Cut several slits in crust with tip of knife.

4   Bake 1 hour or until filling is bubbly and crust is golden brown. Let stand 1 hour before serving.

Deep-Dish Streusel Peach Pie

Makes
6 to 8 servings

1   can (29 ounces) *or* 2 cans (16 ounces each) cling peach slices in syrup

⅓   cup plus 1 tablespoon granulated sugar, divided

1   tablespoon cornstarch

½   teaspoon vanilla

2   cups all-purpose flour, divided

½   cup packed brown sugar

⅓   cup quick oats

¼   cup (½ stick) butter, melted

½   teaspoon ground cinnamon

½   teaspoon salt

½   cup cold shortening, cut into small pieces

4   to 5 tablespoons cold water

Sweetened Whipped Cream (recipe follows)

1   Drain peaches, reserving ¾ cup syrup. Combine ⅓ cup granulated sugar and cornstarch in small saucepan. Gradually add reserved syrup; stir until well blended. Cook and stir over low heat until thickened. Remove from heat; stir in vanilla.

2   Combine ½ cup flour, brown sugar, oats, butter and cinnamon in small bowl; stir until mixture forms coarse crumbs.

3   Preheat oven to 350°F. Combine remaining 1½ cups flour, 1 tablespoon granulated sugar and salt in small bowl. Cut in shortening with pastry blender or two knives until mixture resembles coarse crumbs. Sprinkle water, 1 tablespoon at a time, over flour mixture. Toss lightly with fork until mixture holds together. Shape dough into a ball; flatten into 5- to 6-inch disc.

4 Roll out dough into ⅛-inch-thick square on lightly floured surface. Cut into 10-inch square. Press dough onto bottom and 1 inch up sides of 8-inch square baking dish. Arrange peaches over crust. Pour sauce over peaches. Sprinkle with crumb topping.

5 Bake 45 minutes. Remove to wire rack to cool slightly. Meanwhile, prepare Sweetened Whipped Cream. Serve warm or at room temperature with whipped cream.

Sweetened Whipped Cream: Beat 1 cup cold whipping cream in large bowl with electric mixer at high speed until soft peaks form. Gradually add 3 tablespoons granulated sugar and ½ teaspoon vanilla; beat until stiff peaks form.

All-American Cookie Pie

Makes
8 servings

1 refrigerated pie crust (half of 15-ounce package)
¾ cup (1½ sticks) butter, softened
½ cup granulated sugar
½ cup packed brown sugar
½ teaspoon vanilla
2 eggs
¾ cup all-purpose flour
1 cup (6 ounces) semisweet chocolate chunks or chips
1 cup chopped nuts

1 Preheat oven to 325°F.

2 Line 9-inch pie plate with crust; flute edge.

3 Beat butter, granulated sugar, brown sugar and vanilla in large bowl with electric mixer at medium speed about 3 minutes or until light and fluffy. Add eggs; beat until well blended. Add flour; beat just until blended. Stir in chocolate chunks and nuts. Spread evenly in crust.

4 Bake 65 to 70 minutes or until toothpick inserted into center comes out clean. Cool completely on wire rack.

Cheddar Apple Pie

Makes
8 servings

Single Crust Pie Pastry (recipe follows)

Streusel (recipe follows)

8   cups sliced peeled apples (Rome Beauty, Fuji or Northern Spy)

½   cup packed dark brown sugar

⅓   cup granulated sugar

3   tablespoons all-purpose flour

½   teaspoon ground cinnamon

¼   teaspoon salt

1   cup (4 ounces) shredded sharp Cheddar cheese, divided

1 Prepare Single Crust Pie Pastry and Streusel.

2 Preheat oven to 425°F. Combine apples, brown sugar, granulated sugar, flour, cinnamon and salt in large bowl; toss to coat.

3 Roll out dough into 11-inch circle on floured surface. Sprinkle with ½ cup cheese; roll lightly to adhere. Line 9-inch pie plate with dough; flute edge.

4 Pour apple filling into crust, packing down. Sprinkle with Streusel. Place pie on baking sheet.

5 Bake 15 minutes. *Reduce oven temperature to 350°F.* Loosely cover pie with foil; bake 35 minutes. Remove foil; sprinkle with remaining ½ cup cheese. Bake 10 minutes or until cheese is melted and crust is golden brown. Let stand at least 30 minutes before serving.

Single Crust Pie Pastry: Combine 1¼ cups all-purpose flour and
½ teaspoon salt in medium bowl. Cut in 3 tablespoons cold cubed
shortening and 3 tablespoons cold cubed butter with pastry blender
or two knives until mixture resembles coarse crumbs. Combine
3 tablespoons cold water and ½ teaspoon cider vinegar in small bowl.
Add to flour mixture; mix with fork until dough forms, adding additional
water as needed. Shape dough into a disc; wrap with plastic wrap.
Refrigerate 30 minutes.

Streusel: Combine ⅓ cup all-purpose flour, ⅓ cup granulated sugar,
⅓ cup packed dark brown sugar and ¼ teaspoon salt in medium bowl.
Cut in 5 tablespoons cubed butter with pastry blender or two knives
until mixture resembles coarse crumbs.

Mom's Pumpkin Pie

Makes
16 servings

1½ cans (15 ounces each) solid-pack pumpkin

1 can (12 ounces) evaporated milk

1 cup sugar

2 eggs

2 tablespoons maple syrup

1 teaspoon ground cinnamon

1 teaspoon vanilla

½ teaspoon salt

2 unbaked 9-inch pie crusts

Whipped cream (optional)

1 Preheat oven to 350°F.

2 Combine pumpkin, evaporated milk, sugar, eggs, maple syrup, cinnamon, vanilla and salt in large bowl; mix well. Pour into unbaked crusts. Place pies on baking sheet.

3 Bake 1 hour or until knife inserted into centers comes out clean. Cool completely on wire rack. Top with whipped cream, if desired.

Farmhouse Lemon Meringue Pie

Makes
8 servings

1 unbaked 9-inch pie crust

4 eggs, at room temperature

3 tablespoons lemon juice

2 tablespoons butter, melted

2 teaspoons grated lemon peel

3 drops yellow food coloring (optional)

⅔ cup sugar, divided

1 cup cold water

¼ cup cornstarch

⅛ teaspoon salt

¼ teaspoon vanilla

1 Preheat oven to 425°F. Bake crust according to package directions.

2 Separate eggs; discard two egg yolks. Combine lemon juice, butter, lemon peel and food coloring, if desired, in small bowl; mix well.

3 Reserve 2 tablespoons sugar. Combine water, remaining sugar, cornstarch and salt in medium saucepan; whisk until smooth. Bring to a boil over medium-high heat, whisking constantly. Reduce heat to medium; boil 1 minute, stirring constantly. Remove from heat.

4 Stir ¼ cup boiling sugar mixture into egg yolks; whisk constantly until completely blended. Slowly whisk egg yolk mixture back into boiling sugar mixture. Cook over medium heat 3 minutes, whisking constantly. Remove from heat; stir in lemon juice mixture until well blended. Pour into baked crust.

5 Beat egg whites in large bowl with electric mixer at high speed until soft peaks form. Gradually beat in reserved 2 tablespoons sugar and vanilla; beat until stiff peaks form. Spread meringue over pie filling with rubber spatula, making sure meringue completely covers filling and touches edge of pie crust.

6 Bake 5 to 10 minutes or until meringue is lightly browned. Cool completely on wire rack. Cover with plastic wrap; refrigerate 8 hours or overnight.

Blueberry Pie

Makes
8 servings

Cream Cheese Pastry (recipe follows)
4   cups fresh or thawed frozen blueberries
2   tablespoons cornstarch
⅔   cup blueberry preserves, melted
¼   teaspoon ground nutmeg
1   egg yolk
1   tablespoon sour cream

1 Prepare Cream Cheese Pastry. Preheat oven to 425°F.

2 Roll out one disc of dough into 11-inch circle on floured surface. Line 9-inch pie plate with dough.

3 Combine blueberries and cornstarch in medium bowl; toss gently to coat. Add preserves and nutmeg; mix gently. Pour into crust.

4 Roll out remaining disc of dough into 11-inch circle. Place over filling; turn edge under and flute. Cut several slits or small circles in crust.

5 Bake 10 minutes. *Reduce oven temperature to 350°F.* Beat egg yolk and sour cream in small bowl; brush lightly over crust. Bake 40 minutes or until crust is golden brown. Cool on wire rack 15 minutes. Serve warm, at room temperature or chilled.

Cream Cheese Pastry: Place 1½ cups all-purpose flour in medium bowl. Cut in ½ cup (1 stick) cold cubed butter with pastry blender or two knives until mixture resembles coarse crumbs. Cut in 3 ounces cold cubed cream cheese and 1 teaspoon vanilla until dough forms. Divide dough in half. Shape each half into a disc; wrap with plastic wrap. Refrigerate 30 minutes.

Bourbon Pecan Pie

Makes
6 to 8 servings

Pastry for single-crust 9-inch pie
¼ cup (½ stick) butter, softened
½ cup sugar
3 eggs
1½ cups light or dark corn syrup
2 tablespoons bourbon
1 teaspoon vanilla
1 cup pecan halves

1 Preheat oven to 350°F.

2 Roll out dough to fit 9-inch pie plate; flute edge.

3 Beat butter in large bowl with electric mixer at medium speed until creamy. Add sugar; beat until fluffy. Add eggs, one at a time, beating well after each addition. Add corn syrup, bourbon and vanilla; beat until well blended. Pour into crust; arrange pecans on top.

4 Bake on lowest oven rack 50 to 55 minutes or until knife inserted near center comes out clean. (Filling will be puffy.) Cool completely on wire rack. Serve at room temperature or cover and refrigerate up to 24 hours.

★ Tip: Use your favorite recipe for pie pastry or a frozen deep-dish pie crust.

★ Summer's Best ★

Triple Berry Pie

Makes
8 servings

1 refrigerated pie crust (half of 15-ounce package)

1 lemon

4 cups fresh strawberries, hulled and quartered, divided

½ cup sugar

½ cup water

2 tablespoons cornstarch

1 cup *each* fresh blueberries and fresh raspberries

½ teaspoon vanilla or almond extract

1 Preheat oven to 475°F. Line 9-inch deep-dish pie plate with crust; prick crust all over with fork.

2 Bake 12 minutes or until light golden brown. Remove to wire rack. Finely grate lemon peel over crust; cool completely.

3 Combine 1 cup strawberries, sugar, water and cornstarch in blender; blend until smooth. Pour into large saucepan; bring to a boil over medium-high heat. Boil 1 minute, stirring constantly. Remove from heat; let stand 10 to 15 minutes to cool slightly.

4 Add remaining strawberries, blueberries, raspberries and vanilla to strawberry mixture; stir gently. Pour into crust. Cover with plastic wrap; refrigerate until firm.

Blackberry Custard Pie

Makes
8 servings

Single Crust Pie Pastry (recipe follows)

½ cup sugar

3 tablespoons cornstarch

1¼ cups milk

1 tablespoon lemon juice

2 teaspoons grated lemon peel

2 eggs, lightly beaten

2 cups fresh blackberries

1 Prepare Single Crust Pie Pastry. Preheat oven to 425°F.

2 Roll out dough into 11-inch circle on floured surface. Line 9-inch pie plate with dough; flute edge. Pierce dough with fork at ¼-inch intervals about 40 times. Cut square of foil about 4 inches larger than pie plate. Line crust with foil; fill with dried beans, uncooked rice or ceramic pie weights.

3 Bake 10 minutes or until set. Remove foil lining and beans. Bake 5 minutes or until lightly browned. Cool completely on wire rack.

4 Combine sugar and cornstarch in small saucepan. Add milk, lemon juice and lemon peel; cook and stir over medium heat until mixture boils and thickens. Boil 1 minute, stirring constantly. Stir about ½ cup hot milk mixture into eggs; stir egg mixture back into saucepan. Cook over low heat until thickened, stirring constantly.

5 Pour custard into crust. Cool to room temperature; refrigerate 3 hours or until set. Arrange blackberries over custard.

Single Crust Pie Pastry: Combine 1¼ cups all-purpose flour and ½ teaspoon salt in medium bowl. Cut in 3 tablespoons cold cubed shortening and 3 tablespoons cold cubed butter with pastry blender or two knives until mixture resembles coarse crumbs. Combine 3 tablespoons cold water and ½ teaspoon cider vinegar in small bowl. Add to flour mixture; mix with fork until dough forms, adding additional water as needed. Shape dough into a disc; wrap with plastic wrap. Refrigerate 30 minutes.

Peach Cherry Pie

Makes
6 to 8 servings

1 refrigerated pie crust (half of 15-ounce package)

Streusel Topping (recipe follows)

¾ cup granulated sugar

3 tablespoons quick-cooking tapioca

1 teaspoon grated lemon peel

½ teaspoon ground cinnamon

⅛ teaspoon salt

4 cups sliced peaches (about 7 medium)

2 cups Bing cherries, pitted

1 tablespoon lemon juice

2 tablespoons butter, cut into small pieces

Vanilla ice cream (optional)

1 Let crust stand at room temperature 15 minutes. Preheat oven to 375°F.

2 Prepare Streusel Topping. Line 9-inch pie plate with crust; flute edge.

3 Combine granulated sugar, tapioca, lemon peel, cinnamon and salt in large bowl; mix well. Add peaches, cherries and lemon juice; toss to coat. Pour into crust; dot with butter. Sprinkle streusel over filling.

4 Bake 40 minutes or until filling is bubbly. Cool on wire rack 15 minutes. Serve warm or at room temperature with ice cream, if desired.

Streusel Topping: Combine ¾ cup old-fashioned oats, ⅓ cup all-purpose flour, ⅓ cup packed brown sugar and ¾ teaspoon ground cinnamon in medium bowl. Stir in ¼ cup (½ stick) melted butter until mixture resembles coarse crumbs.

Nectarine Strawberry Pie

Makes
8 servings

Single Crust Pie Pastry (recipe follows)

1½ pounds nectarines, cut into ½-inch-thick slices

½ cup sugar, divided

1 pint fresh strawberries, hulled

1 tablespoon lemon juice

1 tablespoon cornstarch

Whipped cream (optional)

1 Prepare Single Crust Pie Pastry. Preheat oven to 425°F. Reserve 6 to 8 nectarine slices for garnish. Chop remaining nectarines.

2 Roll out dough into 11-inch circle on floured surface. Line 9-inch pie plate with dough; flute edge. Place chopped nectarines in crust; sprinkle with 2 tablespoons sugar. Bake 30 minutes or until fruit is tender and crust is golden brown. Cool on wire rack 30 minutes.

3 Meanwhile, place strawberries in food processor; process until puréed. Press purée through strainer; discard seeds and pulp. Pour liquid into 1-cup measure; add lemon juice and enough water to equal 1 cup.

4 Combine remaining 6 tablespoons sugar and cornstarch in small saucepan. Gradually add strawberry mixture; stir until sugar and cornstarch are dissolved. Bring to a boil over medium heat; cook and stir 5 minutes or until mixture boils and thickens. Remove from heat; cool 15 minutes.

5 Spread strawberry mixture over pie, completely covering nectarines. Cool completely. Refrigerate at least 2 hours or up to 8 hours before serving. Cover with plastic wrap after 1 hour. Top with whipped cream, if desired; garnish with reserved nectarine slices.

Single Crust Pie Pastry: Combine 1¼ cups all-purpose flour and ½ teaspoon salt in medium bowl. Cut in 3 tablespoons cold cubed shortening and 3 tablespoons cold cubed butter with pastry blender or two knives until mixture resembles coarse crumbs. Combine 3 tablespoons cold water and ½ teaspoon cider vinegar in small bowl. Add to flour mixture; mix with fork until dough forms, adding additional water as needed. Shape dough into a disc; wrap with plastic wrap. Refrigerate 30 minutes.

Raspberry Buttermilk Pie

Makes
6 servings

1 unbaked 9-inch deep-dish pie crust

3 eggs, at room temperature

2 tablespoons all-purpose flour

1 cup buttermilk

¾ cup plus 2 tablespoons sugar

¼ cup (½ stick) butter, melted and cooled slightly

¼ cup honey

½ teaspoon vanilla

¼ teaspoon salt

1½ cups fresh raspberries (do not substitute frozen)

1 Preheat oven to 425°F. Place unbaked crust on baking sheet.

2 Bake 5 minutes. (It is not necessary to weigh down crust.) Remove from oven; press down any areas that puff up.

3 *Reduce oven temperature to 350°F.* Beat eggs and flour in large bowl until blended. Beat in buttermilk, sugar, butter, honey, vanilla and salt until sugar is dissolved. Gently stir in raspberries. Pour into crust.

4 Bake 30 minutes. If crust browns before filling is set, loosely cover pie with foil. Bake 20 minutes or until knife inserted near center comes out clean. Let stand 30 minutes before serving.

Rhubarb and Sweet Cherry Pie

Makes
6 to 8 servings

Double Crust Pie Pastry (recipe follows)

4 cups sliced fresh rhubarb (½-inch slices, about 1¼ pounds)

1½ cups fresh or frozen Bing cherries, pitted and cut into halves

1 cup sugar

2 tablespoons cornstarch

½ teaspoon ground cinnamon

⅛ teaspoon salt

2 tablespoons butter, cut into small pieces

1 Prepare Double Crust Pie Pastry. Preheat oven to 400°F.

2 Combine rhubarb and cherries in large bowl. Combine sugar, cornstarch, cinnamon and salt in small bowl; mix well. Add to rhubarb mixture; toss to coat.

3 Roll out one disc of dough into 12-inch circle on floured surface. Line 9-inch pie plate with dough, allowing excess dough to hang over edge.

4 Roll out remaining disc of dough into 11-inch circle on floured surface. Cut into ¾-inch-wide strips.

5 Pour fruit mixture into crust; dot with butter. Arrange dough strips in lattice design over filling. Tuck ends of strips under edge of bottom crust, pressing to seal. Flute edge.

6 Bake about 45 minutes or until rhubarb is tender and filling is bubbly, covering pie loosely with foil during last 10 minutes to prevent overbrowning. Cool on wire rack. Serve warm or at room temperature.

Double Crust Pie Pastry: Combine 2 cups all-purpose flour and 1 teaspoon salt in large bowl. Cut in 6 tablespoons cold cubed shortening and ¼ cup (½ stick) cold cubed butter with pastry blender or two knives until mixture resembles coarse crumbs. Combine 4 tablespoons cold water and ½ teaspoon cider vinegar in small bowl. Add to flour mixture; mix with fork until dough forms, adding additional water as needed. Divide dough in half. Shape each half into a disc; wrap with plastic wrap. Refrigerate 1 hour.

Note: The pie can be prepared using frozen sliced rhubarb. Bake 50 to 55 minutes, covering pie loosely with foil during last 15 minutes of baking to prevent overbrowning.

My Own Berry Pie

Makes
3 servings

1 refrigerated pie crust (half of 15-ounce package)

2 cups fresh or frozen blueberries

2 tablespoons sugar, plus additional for top of pies

2 tablespoons all-purpose flour

1 teaspoon lemon peel

¼ teaspoon vanilla

¼ teaspoon ground cinnamon

1 tablespoon butter, cut into small pieces

1 egg

1 teaspoon water

1 Preheat oven to 375°F. Spray three (4- to 6-ounce) ovenproof jars or ramekins with nonstick cooking spray.

2 Cut crust into six equal pieces. Press one piece into bottom of each prepared jar.

3 Combine blueberries, 2 tablespoons sugar, flour, lemon peel, vanilla and cinnamon in medium bowl; toss gently to coat. Pour into crusts; dot with butter.

4 Cut remaining three pieces of crust into ½-inch strips. Arrange strips in lattice design over top of each jar; press ends of strips securely to seal. Beat egg and water in small bowl; brush over crusts. Sprinkle with additional sugar. Place jars on baking sheet.

5 Bake 40 to 45 minutes or until crusts are golden brown. Let stand 10 to 15 minutes before serving.

Strawberry Cream Pie

Makes
8 servings

1 cup plus ½ tablespoon all-purpose flour, divided

¼ cup plus 1 teaspoon sugar, divided

¼ teaspoon salt

¼ cup (½ stick) cold butter, cut into small pieces

3 tablespoons ice water, divided

¾ teaspoon white or cider vinegar

1 package (8 ounces) cream cheese, softened

¼ cup vanilla yogurt

1 egg

½ teaspoon vanilla

1½ cups fresh strawberries, hulled and halved

¼ cup strawberry jelly

1 Combine 1 cup flour, 1 teaspoon sugar and salt in medium bowl. Cut in butter with pastry blender or two knives until mixture resembles coarse crumbs. Add 2 tablespoons ice water and vinegar; stir until moist but slightly firm dough forms, adding remaining 1 tablespoon water if necessary. Shape dough into a ball.

2 Preheat oven to 450°F. Roll out dough into 12-inch circle on lightly floured surface. Press dough into 9-inch glass pie plate; flute edge. Bake 10 to 12 minutes or until lightly browned. Cool on wire rack. *Reduce oven temperature to 325°F.*

3 Meanwhile, beat cream cheese, remaining ¼ cup sugar and ½ tablespoon flour in large bowl with electric mixer at medium speed until creamy. Beat in yogurt, egg and vanilla until well blended. Pour into crust.

4 Bake 25 minutes or until set. Cool completely on wire rack.

5 Arrange strawberries over filling. Melt jelly in small saucepan over low heat. Carefully brush glaze over strawberries, allowing glaze to run onto cream cheese mixture. Refrigerate 3 hours or overnight.

Peach Raspberry Pie

Makes
6 to 8 servings

Single Crust Pie Pastry (recipe follows)
Almond Crumb Topping (recipe follows)
5   cups sliced peaches (about 2 pounds)
2   tablespoons lemon juice
1   cup fresh raspberries
½   cup sugar
2   tablespoons quick-cooking tapioca
½   teaspoon ground cinnamon
¼   teaspoon ground nutmeg
Whipped cream (optional)

1   Prepare Single-Crust Pie Pastry and Almond Crumb Topping.

2   Preheat oven to 400°F. Roll out dough into 11-inch circle on floured surface. Line 9-inch pie plate with dough; flute edge. Refrigerate 15 minutes.

3   Place peaches in large bowl. Sprinkle with lemon juice; toss to coat. Gently stir in raspberries.

4   Combine sugar, tapioca, cinnamon and nutmeg in small bowl; mix well. Sprinkle over fruit mixture; toss to coat. Pour into crust; sprinkle with Almond Crumb Topping.

5   Bake 15 minutes. *Reduce oven temperature to 350°F.* Bake 30 minutes or until filling is bubbly. Cool on wire rack 15 minutes. Serve warm or at room temperature with whipped cream, if desired.

Single Crust Pie Pastry: Combine 1¼ cups all-purpose flour and ½ teaspoon salt in medium bowl. Cut in 3 tablespoons cold cubed shortening and 3 tablespoons cold cubed butter with pastry blender or two knives until mixture resembles coarse crumbs. Combine 3 tablespoons cold water and ½ teaspoon cider vinegar in small bowl. Add to flour mixture; mix with fork until dough forms, adding additional water as needed. Shape dough into a disc; wrap with plastic wrap. Refrigerate 30 minutes.

Almond Crumb Topping: Combine ⅔ cup old-fashioned or quick oats, ¼ cup all-purpose flour, ¼ cup packed brown sugar, ¼ cup slivered almonds and ½ teaspoon ground cinnamon in medium bowl. Blend in 3 tablespoons softened butter until mixture resembles coarse crumbs.

★ Tip: To substitute frozen fruit, thaw 5 cups frozen sliced peaches in large bowl 1½ to 2 hours. Continue with step 3, using frozen raspberries (do not thaw). Bake as directed in step 5.

Deep-Dish Blueberry Pie

Makes
8 servings

Double Crust Pie Pastry (recipe follows)

- 6 cups fresh blueberries
- 2 tablespoons lemon juice
- 1¼ cups sugar
- 3 tablespoons quick-cooking tapioca
- ¼ teaspoon ground cinnamon
- 1 tablespoon butter, cut into small pieces

1 Prepare Double Crust Pie Pastry. Preheat oven to 400°F.

2 Place blueberries in large bowl; sprinkle with lemon juice. Combine sugar, tapioca and cinnamon in small bowl; mix well. Add to blueberries; toss gently to coat.

3 Roll out one disc of dough into 12-inch circle on lightly floured surface. Line 9-inch deep-dish pie plate with dough; trim all but ½ inch of overhang. Pour blueberry mixture into crust; dot with butter.

4 Roll out remaining disc of dough into 10-inch circle. Cut out four or five shapes from dough with small cookie cutter or knife. Place dough over filling. Trim edge, leaving 1-inch overhang. Fold excess dough under and even with edge of pie plate. Crimp edge with fork.

5 Bake 15 minutes. *Reduce oven temperature to 350°F.* Bake 40 minutes or until crust is golden brown. Cool on wire rack 30 minutes.

Double Crust Pie Pastry: Combine 2½ cups all-purpose flour, 1 teaspoon salt and 1 teaspoon sugar in large bowl. Cut in 1 cup (2 sticks) cold cubed butter with pastry blender or two knives until mixture resembles coarse crumbs. Drizzle ⅓ cup cold water over flour mixture, 2 tablespoons at a time, stirring just until dough forms. Divide dough in half. Shape each half into a disc; wrap with plastic wrap. Refrigerate 30 minutes.

Strawberry Rhubarb Pie

Makes
8 servings

Double Crust Pie Pastry (recipe follows)

1½ cups sugar

½ cup cornstarch

2 tablespoons quick-cooking tapioca

1 tablespoon grated lemon peel

¼ teaspoon ground allspice

4 cups sliced rhubarb (1-inch pieces)

3 cups sliced fresh strawberries

1 egg, lightly beaten

1 Prepare Double Crust Pie Pastry. Preheat oven to 425°F.

2 Roll out one disc of dough into 11-inch circle on floured surface. Line 9-inch pie plate with dough. Combine sugar, cornstarch, tapioca, lemon peel and allspice in large bowl; mix well. Add rhubarb and strawberries; toss to coat. Pour into crust.

3 Roll out remaining disc of dough into 10-inch circle; cut into ½-inch-wide strips. Arrange strips in lattice design over filling; seal and flute edge. Brush crust with beaten egg.

4 Bake 50 minutes or until filling is thick and bubbly and crust is golden brown. Cool on wire rack. Serve warm or at room temperature.

Double Crust Pie Pastry: Combine 2½ cups all-purpose flour, 1 teaspoon salt and 1 teaspoon sugar in large bowl. Cut in 1 cup (2 sticks) cold cubed butter with pastry blender or two knives until mixture resembles coarse crumbs. Drizzle ⅓ cup cold water over flour mixture, 2 tablespoons at a time, stirring just until dough forms. Divide dough in half. Shape each half into a disc; wrap with plastic wrap. Refrigerate 30 minutes.

★ Fall Flavors ★

Maple Walnut Pie

Makes
8 servings

1   cup maple syrup

3   eggs

½   cup packed dark brown sugar

1   tablespoon butter, melted

1   teaspoon vanilla

¼   teaspoon salt

1   cup coarsely chopped walnuts

1   unbaked 9-inch deep-dish pie crust

Whipped cream (optional)

1 Preheat oven to 350°F.

2 Beat maple syrup, eggs, brown sugar, butter, vanilla and salt in large bowl with electric mixer at medium speed until well blended. Stir in walnuts. Pour into unbaked crust.

3 Bake 40 to 45 minutes or until center is set. Cool on wire rack 2 hours. Top with whipped cream, if desired.

Sweet Potato Honey Pie

Makes
8 servings

1 refrigerated pie crust (half of 15-ounce package)

1 can (29 ounces) sweet potatoes, undrained

2 eggs

⅔ cup honey

2 tablespoons butter, melted

¾ teaspoon ground cinnamon

½ teaspoon salt

½ teaspoon ground ginger

¼ teaspoon ground cloves

1 cup whole milk

Whipped cream (optional)

1 Preheat oven to 425°F.

2 Line 9-inch pie plate with crust; flute edge.

3 Drain sweet potatoes, reserving 2 tablespoons syrup. Place sweet potatoes and syrup in food processor; pulse until smooth. Measure 2½ cups; reserve any remaining purée for another use.

4 Beat eggs in large bowl. Add sweet potato purée, honey, butter, cinnamon, salt, ginger and cloves; beat until well blended. Stir in milk. Pour into crust.

5 Bake 15 minutes. *Reduce oven temperature to 350°F.* Bake 40 to 45 minutes or until filling is puffy. Cool on wire rack. Serve at room temperature or chilled. Top with whipped cream, if desired.

Apple-Pear Praline Pie

Makes
8 servings

Double Crust Pie Pastry (recipe follows)

4   cups sliced peeled Granny Smith apples

2   cups sliced peeled pears

¾   cup granulated sugar

¼   cup plus 1 tablespoon all-purpose flour, divided

4   teaspoons ground cinnamon

¼   teaspoon salt

½   cup (1 stick) plus 2 tablespoons butter, divided

1   cup packed brown sugar

1   tablespoon half-and-half

1   cup chopped pecans

1   Prepare Double-Crust Pie Pastry.

2   Combine apples, pears, granulated sugar, ¼ cup flour, cinnamon and salt in large bowl; toss to coat. Let stand 15 minutes.

3   Preheat oven to 350°F. Roll out one disc of dough into 11-inch circle on floured surface. Line 9-inch deep-dish pie plate with dough; sprinkle with remaining 1 tablespoon flour. Pour fruit mixture into crust; dot with 2 tablespoons butter. Roll out remaining disc of dough into 10-inch circle. Place over filling; seal and flute edge. Cut slits in crust with tip of knife. Place pie on baking sheet.

4   Bake 1 hour. Meanwhile, combine remaining ½ cup butter, brown sugar and half-and-half in small saucepan; bring to a boil over medium heat; stirring frequently. Boil 2 minutes, stirring constantly. Remove from heat; stir in pecans. Let stand until thickened to spreadable consistency. Spread over top of pie.

5   Cool on wire rack 15 minutes. Serve warm or at room temperature.

Double Crust Pie Pastry: Combine 2½ cups all-purpose flour, 1 teaspoon salt and 1 teaspoon sugar in large bowl. Cut in 1 cup (2 sticks) cold cubed butter with pastry blender or two knives until coarse crumbs form. Drizzle ⅓ cup cold water over flour mixture, 2 tablespoons at a time, stirring just until dough forms. Divide dough in half. Shape each half into a disc; wrap with plastic wrap. Refrigerate 30 minutes.

Pumpkin Pecan Pie

Makes
8 servings

1 can (15 ounces) solid-pack pumpkin

1 can (14 ounces) sweetened condensed milk

¼ cup (½ stick) butter, softened

2 eggs, divided

1 teaspoon ground cinnamon

1 teaspoon vanilla

½ teaspoon ground nutmeg

¼ teaspoon salt

1 (6-ounce) graham cracker pie crust

2 tablespoons packed brown sugar

2 tablespoons dark corn syrup

1 tablespoon butter, melted

½ teaspoon maple flavoring

1 cup chopped pecans

Whipped cream (optional)

1 Preheat oven to 400°F.

2 Combine pumpkin, sweetened condensed milk, softened butter, 1 egg, cinnamon, vanilla, nutmeg and salt in large bowl; beat until well blended. Pour into crust. Bake 20 minutes.

3 Meanwhile, beat remaining egg, brown sugar, corn syrup, melted butter and maple flavoring in medium bowl with electric mixer at medium speed until well blended. Stir in pecans.

4 Remove pie from oven; top with pecan mixture. *Reduce oven temperature to 350°F.* Bake 25 minutes or until knife inserted near center comes out clean. Cool slightly on wire rack. Serve warm or at room temperature. Top with whipped cream, if desired.

Handheld Apple Pies

Makes
12 servings

2   tablespoons sugar

1   teaspoon ground cinnamon

1   large Granny Smith apple, peeled and coarsely chopped

1   package (about 15 ounces) refrigerated pie crusts (2 crusts)

1 Preheat oven to 350°F. Line two baking sheets with parchment paper.

2 Combine sugar and cinnamon in small bowl. Combine apple and 1 tablespoon cinnamon-sugar in medium bowl; toss to coat.

3 Unroll pie crusts on work surface. Cut out 12 circles with 4-inch round cookie cutter or small bowl. Reserve scraps of dough for decoration, if desired.

4 Place one dough circle on prepared baking sheet. Brush water around edge of dough circle. Place about 2 tablespoons apple mixture on half of circle. Fold dough over filling; press with fork to seal. Repeat with remaining dough circles and apple mixture.

5 Cut out shapes from dough scraps with small cookie cutters, if desired; press onto tops of pies.

6 Bake 20 minutes or until crust is golden brown. Sprinkle remaining cinnamon-sugar over hot pies. Serve warm.

Plum Walnut Pie

Makes
8 servings

Single Crust Pie Pastry (recipe follows)

Oat Streusel (recipe follows)

8   cups thinly sliced plums

⅓   cup granulated sugar

⅓   cup packed brown sugar

3   to 4 tablespoons all-purpose flour

1   tablespoon honey

½   teaspoon ground cinnamon

¼   teaspoon ground ginger

⅛   teaspoon salt

½   cup candied walnuts*

Candied walnuts are sold in packages in the baking section of the supermarket. They may also be found in the produce section where salad ingredients are sold.

1   Prepare Single Crust Pie Pastry and Oat Streusel.

2   Preheat oven to 425°F. Combine plums, granulated sugar, brown sugar, 3 tablespoons flour (use 4 tablespoons if plums are very juicy), honey, cinnamon, ginger and salt in large bowl; toss to coat.

3   Roll out dough into 11-inch circle on floured surface. Line 9-inch pie plate with dough; flute edge. Pour plum mixture into crust; sprinkle with streusel. Place pie on baking sheet.

4   Bake 15 minutes. *Reduce oven temperature to 350°F.* Sprinkle pie with walnuts. Bake 30 minutes. Lightly tent pie with foil; bake 30 minutes or until filling is bubbly and crust and topping are golden brown. Let stand at least 30 minutes before serving.

Single Crust Pie Pastry: Combine 1¼ cups all-purpose flour and ½ teaspoon salt in medium bowl. Cut in 3 tablespoons cold cubed shortening and 3 tablespoons cold cubed butter with pastry blender or two knives until mixture resembles coarse crumbs. Combine 3 tablespoons cold water and ½ teaspoon cider vinegar in small bowl. Add to flour mixture; mix with fork just until dough forms, adding additional water as needed. Shape dough into a disc; wrap with plastic wrap. Refrigerate 30 minutes.

Oat Streusel: Combine ¼ cup all-purpose flour, ¼ cup old-fahioned oats, ¼ cup granulated sugar, ¼ cup packed brown sugar and ⅛ teaspoon salt in medium bowl. Add ¼ cup (½ stick) cold cubed butter; mix with fingertips until mixture resembles coarse crumbs.

Sweet Potato Pecan Pie

Makes
8 servings

1   unbaked 9-inch deep-dish pie crust

1½   cups pecan halves

½   cup light corn syrup

1   egg white

2   cups puréed cooked sweet potatoes (about 1½ pounds
      uncooked sweet potatoes)

⅓   cup packed brown sugar

1   teaspoon vanilla

½   teaspoon ground cinnamon

¼   teaspoon salt

     Pinch ground nutmeg

     Pinch ground cloves

2   eggs, beaten

     Whipped cream (optional)

1   Preheat oven to 400°F.

2   Prick holes in bottom of unbaked crust with fork. Bake 10 minutes or until lightly browned. Cool completely on wire rack.

3   *Reduce oven temperature to 350°F.* Combine pecans, corn syrup and egg white in small bowl; mix well. Beat sweet potatoes, brown sugar, vanilla, cinnamon, salt, nutmeg and cloves in large bowl until well blended. Beat in eggs until blended. Pour into crust; top with pecan mixture.

4   Bake 45 minutes or until filling is puffed and topping is golden brown. Cool completely on wire rack. Top with whipped cream, if desired.

Ginger-Spiced Pumpkin Pie

Makes
8 servings

1 cup finely crushed gingersnap cookies

¼ cup (½ stick) butter, melted

2 egg whites

¾ cup packed brown sugar

1 can (15 ounces) solid-pack pumpkin

1 cup evaporated milk

1 teaspoon vanilla

1 teaspoon ground ginger

1 teaspoon ground cinnamon

½ teaspoon salt

Additional gingersnap cookies (optional)

1 Combine crushed cookies and butter in medium bowl; mix well. Press onto bottom and up side of 9-inch deep-dish pie plate. Refrigerate 30 minutes.

2 Preheat oven to 350°F. Beat egg whites and brown sugar in large bowl. Add pumpkin, evaporated milk, vanilla, ginger, cinnamon and salt; beat until well blended. Pour into crust.

3 Bake 60 to 70 minutes or until center is set. Remove to wire rack; cool 30 minutes. Serve warm or at room temperature. Garnish with additional cookies, if desired.

Cranberry Apple Nut Pie

Makes
8 servings

Rich Pie Pastry (recipe follows)

1 cup sugar

3 tablespoons all-purpose flour

¼ teaspoon salt

4 cups sliced peeled tart apples (4 large apples)

2 cups fresh cranberries

½ cup golden raisins

½ cup coarsely chopped pecans

1 tablespoon grated lemon peel

2 tablespoons butter, cut into small pieces

1 egg, beaten

1 Prepare Rich Pie Pastry. Preheat oven to 425°F.

2 Roll out one disc of dough into 11-inch circle on floured surface. Line 9-inch pie plate with dough.

3 Combine sugar, flour and salt in large bowl; mix well. Stir in apples, cranberries, raisins, pecans and lemon peel; toss to coat. Pour into crust; dot with butter.

4 Roll out remaining disc of dough into 11-inch circle. Place over filling; trim excess dough. Seal and flute edge. Cut slits in crust with tip of knife. Lightly brush crust with egg.

5 Bake 35 minutes or until apples are tender when pierced with fork and crust is golden brown. Cool on wire rack 15 minutes. Serve warm or cool completely.

Rich Pie Pastry: Combine 2 cups all-purpose flour and ¼ teaspoon salt in medium bowl. Cut in 6 tablespoons cold cubed butter and 6 tablespoons cold cubed shortening with pastry blender or two knives until mixture resembles coarse crumbs. Drizzle 6 tablespoons cold water, 1 tablespoon at a time, over flour mixture, stirring just until dough forms. Divide dough in half. Shape each half into a disc; wrap with plastic wrap. Refrigerate 30 minutes.

Sour Cream Squash Pie

Makes
8 servings

1 package (12 ounces) frozen winter squash, thawed and drained

½ cup sour cream

¼ cup sugar

1 egg

1½ teaspoons pumpkin pie spice

½ teaspoon salt

½ teaspoon vanilla

¾ cup evaporated milk

1 (9-inch) graham cracker pie crust

¼ cup chopped hazelnuts, toasted* (optional)

To toast hazelnuts, spread on baking sheet. Bake at 350°F 7 to 10 minutes or until light golden brown, stirring occasionally. Immediately remove from pan; cool completely before using.

1 Preheat oven to 350°F.

2 Beat squash, sour cream, sugar, egg, pumpkin pie spice, salt and vanilla in large bowl until well blended. Beat in evaporated milk until blended. Pour into crust.

3 Bake 1 hour and 10 minutes or until set. Cool completely on wire rack. Sprinkle with hazelnuts just before serving, if desired.

Maple-Sweet Potato Cheesecake Pies

Makes
12 servings

1 package (8 ounces) reduced-fat cream cheese
   (such as Neufchâtel), softened

½ cup vanilla yogurt

1 can (16 ounces) sweet potatoes, drained and mashed

½ cup pure maple syrup

1 teaspoon vanilla

½ teaspoon ground cinnamon

¼ teaspoon ground cloves

1 egg

1 egg white

12 mini graham cracker crusts

12 pecan halves

1 Preheat oven to 350°F.

2 Beat cream cheese in large bowl with electric mixer at medium speed until creamy. Add yogurt; beat until smooth. Add sweet potatoes, maple syrup, vanilla, cinnamon and cloves; beat until well blended. Beat in egg and egg white until blended.

3 Spoon about ⅓ cup sweet potato mixture into each crust. Top with pecan half. Place filled crusts on large baking sheet.

4 Bake 30 to 35 minutes or until set and knife inserted into centers comes out clean. Cool on wire rack 1 hour. Refrigerate until ready to serve.

Variation: Pour sweet potato mixture into 9-inch graham cracker crust. Bake 40 to 45 minutes.

Chocoholics' Delight

Chocolate Cookie Pie

Makes
8 servings

1 cup whipping cream
20 chocolate sandwich cookies, divided
1 (6-ounce) chocolate crumb pie crust, divided

1 Beat cream in large bowl with electric mixer at high speed until soft peaks form.

2 Place 14 cookies in resealable food storage bag; crush into coarse crumbs with rolling pin or mallet.

3 Stir crumbs into whipped cream; spread evenly in crust. Garnish with remaining cookies. Cover and freeze until ready to serve. Let stand at room temperature 10 minutes before serving.

Chocolate Chess Pie

Makes
8 servings

4 squares (1 ounce each) unsweetened chocolate

3 tablespoons butter

3 eggs

1 egg yolk

1¼ cups sugar

½ cup half-and-half

1 to 2 teaspoons instant coffee granules

¼ teaspoon salt

1 unbaked 9-inch pie crust

Whipped cream

Chocolate-covered coffee beans (optional)

1 Preheat oven to 325°F.

2 Combine chocolate and butter in small heavy saucepan; heat over low heat until melted, stirring frequently. Let stand 15 minutes.

3 Beat eggs and egg yolk in medium bowl. Add sugar, half-and-half, coffee granules and salt; beat until blended. Beat in chocolate mixture until smooth. Pour into unbaked crust.

4 Bake 35 minutes or until set. Cool completely on wire rack. Refrigerate 2 hours or until ready to serve. Top with whipped cream; garnish with chocolate-covered coffee beans.

Note: Use 2 teaspoons instant coffee granules for a more pronounced coffee flavor; use a smaller amount if a more subtle coffee flavor is preferred.

Chocolate Velvet Pie

Makes
10 servings

1 unbaked 9-inch deep-dish pie crust

4 ounces semisweet chocolate

¾ cup half-and-half

3 eggs, divided

1 egg yolk

10 tablespoons sugar, divided

1 teaspoon vanilla, divided

⅛ teaspoon salt

1 package (8 ounces) cream cheese, softened

¼ cup whipping cream

Fresh raspberries and semisweet chocolate curls (optional)

1 Preheat oven to 400°F. Prick holes in bottom of unbaked crust with fork. Bake 10 minutes or until lightly browned. Cool completely on wire rack.

2 *Reduce oven temperature to 350°F.* Combine chocolate and half-and-half in medium heavy saucepan; heat over low heat until chocolate is melted, stirring frequently. Remove from heat.

3 Beat 2 eggs and egg yolk in small bowl. Beat into chocolate mixture until blended. Add 6 tablespoons sugar, ½ teaspoon vanilla and salt; beat until well blended. Pour into crust.

4 Beat cream cheese and remaining 4 tablespoons sugar in medium bowl with electric mixer at medium-high speed until smooth. Add cream, remaining egg and ½ teaspoon vanilla; beat until well blended. Gently drop cream cheese mixture by spoonfuls over chocolate filling; spread to cover surface of pie.

5 Bake 40 minutes or until set. Cool completely on wire rack. Cover and refrigerate at least 2 hours before serving. Garnish with raspberries and chocolate curls.

Chocolate Caramel Surprise Pie

Makes
8 to 10 servings

1½ cups plus 6 tablespoons whipping cream, divided

8 ounces semisweet chocolate, chopped, divided

1 (6-ounce) chocolate crumb pie crust

¼ cup caramel dessert topping

6 tablespoons sugar, divided

¼ teaspoon salt

3 egg yolks

½ teaspoon vanilla

Whipped cream and caramels (optional)

1 Combine ½ cup cream and 4 ounces chocolate in small heavy saucepan; heat over low heat until chocolate is melted, stirring frequently. Cool slightly. Spread evenly in crust. Refrigerate 30 minutes. Spread caramel topping over chocolate layer. Refrigerate 30 minutes.

2 Combine 1 cup cream and remaining 4 ounces chocolate in same saucepan; heat over low heat until chocolate is melted, stirring frequently. Stir in 4 tablespoons sugar and salt; cool slightly.

3 Beat egg yolks in small bowl. Pour ½ cup chocolate mixture into egg yolks, stirring constantly. Pour egg mixture back into saucepan; cook and stir over low heat until thickened. Cook and stir 1 minute. (Mixture should reach 160°F.) Pour into large bowl; stir in vanilla. Refrigerate 30 minutes, stirring occasionally.

4 Beat remaining 6 tablespoons cream and 2 tablespoons sugar in small bowl with electric mixer at high speed until stiff peaks form. Fold whipped cream into chocolate mixture. Gently spread over caramel layer. Refrigerate 4 hours or overnight. Top with whipped topping and caramels, if desired.

Fudgy Brownie Pie

Makes
12 servings

12	squares (1 ounce each) bittersweet chocolate*
½	cup (1 stick) butter
2	eggs
½	cup sugar
1	cup all-purpose flour
½	teaspoon salt
	Vanilla ice cream
	Hot fudge topping, heated
	Maraschino cherries (optional)

Or substitute 4 squares unsweetened chocolate and 8 squares semisweet chocolate.

1 Preheat oven to 350°F.

2 Grease 10-inch tart pan with removable bottom or 9-inch square baking pan.

3 Combine chocolate and butter in small heavy saucepan; heat over low heat until melted, stirring frequently.

4 Beat eggs in medium bowl with electric mixer at medium speed 30 seconds. Gradually add sugar; beat 1 minute. Add chocolate mixture; beat until blended, scraping down side of bowl once. Add flour and salt; beat at low speed just until combined. Spread evenly in prepared pan.

5 Bake 25 minutes or just until center is set. Cool completely on wire rack. Top with ice cream, hot fudge and cherry, if desired.

Chocolate Mint Pie

Makes
8 servings

30 marshmallows

½ cup milk

4 ounces bittersweet chocolate, finely chopped

2 ounces unsweetened chocolate, finely chopped

½ teaspoon mint extract

1½ cups whipping cream

1 (6-ounce) chocolate crumb pie crust

1 container (8 ounces) whipped topping

12 chocolate mint sandwich cookies, chopped

1 Combine marshmallows and milk in medium saucepan; cook over medium heat 7 minutes or until melted and smooth, stirring constantly. Remove from heat; stir in chopped chocolate and mint extract until chocolate is melted and mixture is smooth.

2 Beat cream in large bowl with electric mixer at medium speed until stiff peaks form. Fold one fourth of whipped cream into chocolate mixture just until lightened. Fold chocolate mixture into remaining whipped cream until blended. Spread evenly in crust.

3 Spread whipped topping over chocolate layer; sprinkle with cookie pieces. Refrigerate at least 3 hours or overnight.

Chocolate Peanut Pie

Makes
8 servings

1½ cups all-purpose flour

½ cup plus 1 tablespoon sugar, divided

½ teaspoon salt, divided

½ cup (1 stick) butter, melted

¾ cup half-and-half

½ cup semisweet chocolate chips

3 eggs

½ teaspoon vanilla

½ cup caramel dessert topping

¾ cup honey-roasted peanuts

1 Preheat oven to 425°F. Combine flour, 1 tablespoon sugar and ¼ teaspoon salt in medium bowl. Gradually add melted butter, stirring until dough forms.

2 Place dough in 9-inch pie plate; press onto bottom and up side to form high rim. Place on baking sheet. Bake 5 minutes. (It is not necessary to weigh down crust.)

3 *Reduce oven temperature to 350°F.* Combine half-and-half and chocolate chips in medium heavy saucepan; heat over low heat until chocolate is melted, stirring frequently. Remove from heat; stir in remaining ½ cup sugar and ¼ teaspoon salt. Beat in eggs, one at a time, until blended. Stir in vanilla.

4 Spread caramel topping evenly over bottom of crust; sprinkle with peanuts. Gently spoon chocolate mixture over peanuts. (Most peanuts will float to top.)

5 Bake 45 minutes or until set. Cool on wire rack 15 minutes. Refrigerate at least 4 hours or overnight.

Fancy Fudge Pie

Makes
8 servings

1 cup chocolate wafer crumbs

⅓ cup butter, melted

1⅓ cups (8 ounces) semisweet chocolate chips

¾ cup packed brown sugar

½ cup (1 stick) butter, softened

3 eggs

1 cup chopped pecans

½ cup all-purpose flour

1 teaspoon vanilla

½ teaspoon instant espresso powder

Whipped cream (optional)

Chocolate syrup (optional)

1 Preheat oven to 375°F. Combine chocolate crumbs and melted butter in small bowl; mix well. Press onto bottom and up side of 9-inch pie plate. Bake 5 minutes. Cool completely on wire rack.

2 Place chocolate chips in small microwavable bowl. Microwave on HIGH 1 minute or until melted and smooth. Cool slightly.

3 Beat brown sugar and softened butter in large bowl with electric mixer at medium speed until light and fluffy. Add eggs, one at a time, beating well after each addition. Stir in melted chocolate, pecans, flour, vanilla and espresso powder until well blended. Pour into crust.

4 Bake 30 minutes or until set. Cool completely on wire rack. Cover and refrigerate 2 hours or until ready to serve. Garnish with whipped cream and chocolate syrup.

Italian Chocolate Pie alla Lucia

Makes
8 servings

¼ cup pine nuts

3 tablespoons packed brown sugar

1 tablespoon grated orange peel

1 unbaked 9-inch pie crust

4 ounces bittersweet chocolate, coarsely chopped

3 tablespoons butter

1 can (5 ounces) evaporated milk

3 eggs

3 tablespoons hazelnut liqueur

1 teaspoon vanilla

Whipped cream and bittersweet chocolate curls (optional)

1 Toast pine nuts in dry nonstick skillet over medium heat, stirring constantly until golden brown and fragrant. Remove from heat. Finely chop pine nuts; set aside to cool completely.

2 Combine pine nuts, brown sugar and orange peel in small bowl; mix well. Sprinkle over bottom of unbaked crust; gently press into crust.

3 Preheat oven to 325°F. Combine chocolate and butter in small heavy saucepan; heat over low heat until melted, stirring frequently. Cool to room temperature.

4 Beat chocolate mixture and evaporated milk in medium bowl with electric mixer at medium speed until blended. Add eggs, one at a time, beating well after each addition. Stir in hazelnut liqueur and vanilla. Pour into crust.

5 Bake in center of oven 30 to 40 minutes or until set. Cool completely on wire rack. Refrigerate until ready to serve. Top with whipped cream and chocolate curls, if desired.

★ Cool & Creamy ★

Chilly Lemon Pie

Makes
8 servings

1¼ cups graham cracker crumbs (about 1 package)

¼ cup (½ stick) butter, melted

1 tablespoon sugar

1 tablespoon plus 1 teaspoon grated lemon peel, divided

1 can (14 ounces) sweetened condensed milk

½ cup lemon juice (about 3 lemons)

Lemon slices and fresh raspberries (optional)

1 Preheat oven to 350°F.

2 Combine graham cracker crumbs, butter, sugar and 1 teaspoon lemon peel in 9-inch pie plate; mix well. Press onto bottom and up side of pie plate.

3 Bake 7 to 10 minutes or until golden brown. Cool completely on wire rack.

4 Whisk sweetened condensed milk, lemon juice and remaining 1 tablespoon lemon peel in medium bowl until well blended. Pour into crust. Cover and refrigerate 3 hours or until set. Garnish with lemon slices and raspberries.

Cherry Cheesecake Pie

Makes
8 to 10 servings

12   whole graham crackers, crushed into crumbs

¼   cup (½ stick) butter, melted

3   tablespoons sugar, divided

1   can (21 ounces) cherry pie filling, divided

1   package (¼ ounce) unflavored gelatin

¼   cup cold water

¾   cup boiling water

1   package (8 ounces) cream cheese, softened

1   teaspoon vanilla

½   (8-ounce) container thawed frozen whipped topping

Semisweet chocolate shavings (optional)

1   Preheat oven to 350°F. Combine graham cracker crumbs, butter and 1 tablespoon sugar in medium bowl; mix well. Press onto bottom and up side of 9-inch deep-dish pie plate. Bake 8 to 10 minutes. Cool completely on wire rack.

2   Spread two thirds of pie filling over crust. Cover and refrigerate remaining filling until ready to serve.

3   Combine gelatin and cold water in small bowl; let stand 5 minutes to soften. Add boiling water; stir until gelatin is completely dissolved. Cool mixture 5 to 10 minutes.

4   Beat cream cheese, remaining 2 tablespoons sugar and vanilla in large bowl with electric mixer at medium speed until smooth. Slowly add ¾ cup gelatin mixture (discard remaining ¼ cup gelatin mixture); beat at low speed until blended. Stir in half of whipped topping until smooth. Pour cream cheese mixture over cherry filling in crust. Cover and refrigerate at least 3 hours or until firm. Top with remaining pie filling and whipped topping. Garnish with chocolate shavings.

Banana Cream Pie

Makes
8 servings

1 unbaked 9-inch pie crust

3 bananas, divided

1 teaspoon lemon juice

½ cup sugar

6 tablespoons cornstarch

¼ teaspoon salt

3 cups milk

2 egg yolks

1½ teaspoons vanilla

Whipped cream and ground cinnamon (optional)

1 Preheat oven to 400°F.

2 Prick holes in bottom of unbaked crust with fork. Bake 10 minutes or until lightly browned. Cool on wire rack 15 minutes.

3 Slice 2 bananas; toss with lemon juice in medium bowl. Arrange in single layer on bottom of crust.

4 Combine sugar, cornstarch and salt in medium saucepan; mix well. Beat milk and egg yolks in medium bowl; slowly stir into sugar mixture. Cook and stir over medium heat until thickened. Boil 1 minute, stirring constantly. Remove from heat; stir in vanilla. Pour into crust; immediately cover with waxed paper. Refrigerate 2 hours or until ready to serve.

5 Slice remaining banana; arrange slices around edge of pie. Garnish with whipped cream and cinnamon.

Mocha Decadence Pie

Makes
8 servings

4 ounces semisweet chocolate, chopped

2 cups whipping cream, divided

½ cup plus 1 tablespoon sugar, divided

3 eggs

2 teaspoons instant coffee granules

1 teaspoon vanilla, divided

1 (6-ounce) graham cracker pie crust

Semisweet chocolate shavings (optional)

1 Place chocolate in small microwavable bowl; microwave on HIGH 1½ minutes or until melted, stirring after 1 minute. Set aside.

2 Combine 1 cup cream and ½ cup sugar in medium saucepan; cook and stir over medium heat until sugar is dissolved. Beat eggs in small bowl; stir in ¼ cup cream mixture. Pour egg mixture back into cream mixture; cook 4 to 5 minutes or until thickened, stirring constantly. Pour into large bowl.

3 Add melted chocolate, coffee granules and ½ teaspoon vanilla; beat with electric mixer at low speed until blended. Beat at medium speed 2 minutes. Pour into crust. Cool 15 minutes. Cover and refrigerate 3 hours or overnight.

4 Beat remaining 1 cup cream in medium bowl with electric mixer at high speed 1 minute. Add remaining 1 tablespoon sugar and ½ teaspoon vanilla; beat until soft peaks form. Top pie with whipped cream; garnish with chocolate shavings.

Lemon Chess Pie

Makes
8 servings

1 refrigerated pie crust (half of 15-ounce package)

3 eggs

2 egg yolks

1¾ cups sugar

½ cup half-and-half

⅓ cup lemon juice

¼ cup (½ stick) butter, melted

3 tablespoons grated lemon peel, plus additional for garnish

2 tablespoons all-purpose flour

Whipped cream (optional)

1 Let crust stand at room temperature 15 minutes. Preheat oven to 325°F.

2 Line 9-inch pie plate with crust; flute edge.

3 Beat eggs and egg yolks in large bowl. Add sugar, half-and-half, lemon juice, butter, 3 tablespoons lemon peel and flour; beat until well blended. Pour into crust.

4 Bake 40 minutes or until almost set. Cool completely on wire rack. Refrigerate 2 hours or until ready to serve. Top with whipped cream, if desired; garnish with additional lemon peel.

Note: To determine doneness, carefully shake pie. It is done when only the center 2 inches jiggle.

Black Bottom Pie

Makes
8 servings

1 package (¼ ounce) unflavored gelatin

¼ cup cold water

⅔ cup semisweet chocolate chips

½ cup granulated sugar

1 tablespoon cornstarch

¼ teaspoon salt

3 cups whipping cream, divided

3 eggs

1 (6-ounce) chocolate graham cracker pie crust

1 to 2 tablespoons rum

3 tablespoons powdered sugar

Grated chocolate (optional)

1 Sprinkle gelatin over ¼ cup cold water in cup; let stand until ready to use. Place chocolate chips in medium bowl.

2 Combine granulated sugar, cornstarch and salt in medium heavy saucepan; mix well. Gradually add 1½ cups cream, stirring constantly. Add eggs; stir until well blended. Cook over low heat 10 to 12 minutes or until thickened, stirring constantly. (Custard should coat back of spoon. Run fingertip across back of spoon; if mark remains, custard is ready.)

3 Pour half of hot custard over chocolate chips; let stand 1 minute. Stir until chocolate is melted and mixture is smooth. Pour into crust; refrigerate 45 minutes.

4 Add gelatin mixture to remaining custard; stir about 30 seconds. Stir in ¾ cup cream and rum until well blended. Refrigerate 45 to 60 minutes or until thickened but not set.

5   Beat rum custard in medium bowl with electric mixer at high
speed 5 minutes or until smooth and fluffy. Spread over
chocolate layer in crust.

6   Beat remaining ¾ cup cream and powdered sugar in large bowl
with electric mixer at high speed until stiff peaks form. Spread
over rum custard layer. Refrigerate at least 1 hour or until ready
to serve. Garnish with grated chocolate.

Cool & Creamy   ★

Spiced Raisin Custard Pie

Makes
12 servings

1½ cups raisins

½ cup plus 1 teaspoon sugar, divided

1 tablespoon ground cinnamon, divided

1 can (14 ounces) sweetened condensed milk

1 cup biscuit baking mix

1 cup applesauce

3 eggs

¼ cup (½ stick) butter, melted

2 teaspoons vanilla

1 teaspoon ground nutmeg

1 container (8 ounces) thawed frozen whipped topping

1 Preheat oven to 325°F. Spray 10-inch glass pie plate with nonstick cooking spray.

2 Place raisins in medium bowl. Combine 1 teaspoon sugar and 1 teaspoon cinnamon in small bowl; reserve half for top of pie. Sprinkle remaining cinnamon-sugar over raisins; toss to coat.

3 Combine sweetened condensed milk, baking mix, applesauce, eggs, remaining ½ cup sugar, butter, vanilla, remaining 2 teaspoons cinnamon and nutmeg in large bowl; beat with electric mixer at medium speed 2 minutes or until well blended. Pour into prepared pie plate.

4 Bake 10 minutes. Remove from oven; top with spiced raisins and sprinkle with reserved cinnamon-sugar. Bake 35 to 40 minutes (center will be soft). Cool to room temperature; refrigerate at least 2 hours. Serve chilled with whipped topping.

Creamy Peanut Butter Pie

Makes
8 servings

1 cup creamy peanut butter, divided

2 tablespoons corn syrup

1 tablespoon butter

1 (6-ounce) graham cracker pie crust

1 (2-ounce) chocolate-covered crunchy peanut butter candy bar, crushed, divided

1⅔ cups cold milk

2 packages (4-serving size each) vanilla instant pudding and pie filling mix

1 container (8 ounces) thawed frozen whipped topping, divided

1 Combine ¾ cup peanut butter, corn syrup and butter in medium microwavable bowl. Microwave on HIGH 1 minute; stir until smooth. Spread evenly over bottom of crust; sprinkle with 6 tablespoons crushed candy bar.

2 Beat milk and pudding mix in medium bowl with electric mixer at low speed 2 minutes or until thickened. Beat in remaining ¼ cup peanut butter until blended.

3 Remove ½ cup whipped topping from container; set aside. Fold remaining whipped topping into pudding mixture until blended. Spread over peanut butter layer in crust. Top with reserved whipped topping; sprinkle with remaining crushed candy bar. Refrigerate until ready to serve.

Amaretto Coconut Cream Pie

Makes
8 servings

¼ cup flaked coconut

1 container (8 ounces) thawed frozen whipped topping, divided

1 container (6 ounces) coconut or vanilla yogurt

¼ cup amaretto liqueur

1 package (4-serving size) coconut instant pudding and pie filling mix

1 (6-ounce) graham cracker pie crust

Fresh strawberries and fresh mint leaves (optional)

1 Preheat oven to 350°F.

2 Spread coconut in even layer on baking sheet. Bake 5 minutes or until golden brown, stirring frequently. Cool completely.

3 Combine 2 cups whipped topping, yogurt and amaretto in large bowl; stir until blended. Add pudding mix; whisk 2 minutes or until thickened.

4 Spread evenly in crust; spread remaining whipped topping over filling. Sprinkle with toasted coconut. Refrigerate until ready to serve. Garnish with strawberries and mint.

Frozen Treats

Dreamy Orange Pie

Makes
8 servings

8   whole honey graham crackers, crushed (1½ cups)

2   tablespoons butter, melted

1   pint vanilla ice cream, softened

1   pint orange sherbet, softened

   Whipped cream (optional)

   Mandarin orange slices (optional)

1   Preheat oven to 350°F. Spray 9-inch springform pan with nonstick cooking spray.

2   Combine graham cracker crumbs and butter in medium bowl; mix well. Press onto bottom and ½ inch up side of prepared pan. Bake 8 to 10 minutes or until lightly browned. Cool completely on wire rack.

3   Spread ice cream evenly in crust. Freeze 30 minutes or until firm to the touch. Spread orange sherbet over ice cream; freeze at least 1 hour or until firm.

4   Carefully run knife around edge of pan; remove side of pan. Top with whipped cream and orange slices, if desired.

Leftover Candy Ice Cream Pie

Makes
10 servings

Brown Sugar Crumb Crust (recipe follows)

2 cups vanilla ice cream

½ cup chocolate sauce, divided

8 snack-size chocolate candy bars,* chopped, divided

2 cups chocolate ice cream

¾ cup whipping cream, whipped

Use your favorite candy bars.

1 Prepare Brown Sugar Crumb Crust.

2 Let vanilla ice cream stand at room temperature about 5 minutes or just until softened; spread evenly in crust. Drizzle with ¼ cup chocolate sauce; sprinkle with half of chopped candy bars. Freeze 1½ hours or until firm.

3 Let chocolate ice cream stand at room temperature about 5 minutes or just until softened; spread evenly over chopped candy bars. Drizzle with remaining ¼ cup chocolate sauce. Freeze 6 hours or until firm.

4 Let pie stand in refrigerator 20 minutes before serving. Spread whipped cream over pie; sprinkle with remaining chopped candy bars.

Brown Sugar Crumb Crust: Preheat oven to 350°F. Combine 1¼ cups graham cracker crumbs, 2 tablespoons packed brown sugar and ⅓ cup melted butter in large bowl; mix well. Press onto bottom and up side of 9-inch pie plate. Bake 8 to 10 minutes or until edges are golden brown. Cool completely on wire rack.

Easy Cherry Cream Pie

Makes
8 servings

1 pint vanilla ice cream, softened

½ (16-ounce) package frozen dark sweet cherries, chopped

1 cup whipping cream

1 tablespoon powdered sugar

⅛ teaspoon almond extract

1 (6-ounce) chocolate crumb or graham cracker pie crust

1 Combine ice cream and cherries in large bowl; stir just until blended.

2 Beat cream, sugar and almond extract in medium bowl with electric mixer at medium-high speed until soft peaks form.

3 Spread ice cream evenly in crust. Spread whipped cream over ice cream. Freeze 1 hour or until firm. Let stand at room temperature 10 minutes before serving.

Pistachio Ice Cream Pie

Makes
8 servings

1 jar (12 ounces) hot fudge dessert topping, divided
1 (6-ounce) chocolate crumb pie crust
2 pints pistachio ice cream, softened
½ cup chopped pistachio nuts

1 Spread half of hot fudge topping over bottom of crust; freeze 10 minutes.

2 Spread ice cream evenly over fudge topping; sprinkle with chopped pistachios. Cover and freeze 2 hours or until firm.

3 Let pie stand at room temperature 10 minutes before serving. Heat remaining fudge topping according to package directions; serve with pie.

Chocolate Peanut Butter Pie

Makes
6 to 8 servings

1   can (14 ounces) sweetened condensed milk

¼   cup creamy peanut butter

2   tablespoons unsweetened cocoa powder

1   container (8 ounces) thawed frozen whipped topping,
    plus additional for serving

1   (6-ounce) chocolate crumb pie crust

1   Beat sweetened condensed milk, peanut butter and cocoa in large bowl with electric mixer at medium speed until smooth and well blended.

2   Fold in one container of whipped topping until blended. Pour into crust. Freeze at least 6 hours or overnight.

3   Let pie stand at room temperature 10 minutes before serving. Top with additional whipped topping, if desired.

Crunchy Ice Cream Pie

Makes
6 servings

8 ounces semisweet chocolate, chopped

2 tablespoons butter

1½ cups crisp rice cereal

½ gallon chocolate chip or fudge ripple ice cream, softened

Hot fudge dessert topping

1 Spray 9-inch pie plate with nonstick cooking spray.

2 Combine chocolate and butter in medium heavy saucepan; heat over low heat until melted, stirring frequently. Remove from heat. Add cereal; stir until well blended. Spoon into prepared pie plate; press onto bottom and up side to form crust.

3 Spread ice cream evenly in crust. Cover and freeze until ready to serve.

4 Let pie stand at room temperature 10 minutes before serving. Drizzle with hot fudge topping.

Strawberry Sundae Pie

Makes
9 servings

¼ cup creamy peanut butter

3 tablespoons light corn syrup

2 cups crisp rice cereal

1¾ cups chocolate frozen yogurt, slightly softened

1½ cups strawberry or raspberry sorbet

Sliced fresh strawberries (optional)

1 Spray 9-inch pie plate with nonstick cooking spray.

2 Combine peanut butter and corn syrup in medium bowl; mix well. Stir in cereal until coated. Press onto bottom and up side of prepared pie plate. Loosely cover and refrigerate 15 minutes.

3 Spread frozen yogurt in crust. Use small ice cream scoop to scoop sorbet into small balls onto yogurt layer. Cover and freeze about 2 hours or until firm.

4 Let pie stand at room temperature 10 minutes before serving. Garnish with strawberries.

Mexican Ice Cream Pie

Makes
6 to 8 servings

1 cup butter pecan ice cream, softened

1 (6-ounce) chocolate crumb pie crust

½ cup caramel dessert topping

2 cups coffee ice cream, softened

1 jar (12 ounces) hot fudge dessert topping

½ cup coffee liqueur (optional)

1 Spread butter pecan ice cream evenly in crust. Freeze 20 minutes or until almost firm.

2 Spread caramel topping over butter pecan ice cream. Freeze 20 minutes or until firm.

3 Spread coffee ice cream over caramel topping. Freeze 6 hours or overnight.

4 Combine hot fudge topping and coffee liqueur, if desired, in small saucepan; cook and stir over medium heat until heated through.

5 Let pie stand at room temperature 10 minutes before serving. Drizzle with hot fudge mixture.

Easy Berry Pie

Makes
8 servings

1   (6-ounce) graham cracker pie crust

1½   cups milk

1   package (4-serving size) cheesecake or vanilla instant pudding and pie filling mix

2   teaspoons grated lemon peel

3   cups fresh strawberries, hulled

½   cup fresh blueberries

1   tablespoon sugar

    Whipped cream (optional)

1   Preheat oven to 375°F.

2   Bake crust 5 minutes; cool completely on wire rack.

3   Pour milk into medium bowl. Whisk in pudding mix 1 minute or until mixture is thick. Stir in lemon peel. Pour filling into crust. Cover and refrigerate at least 3 hours.

4   Cut strawberries into halves (or quarters if berries are large). Combine strawberries and blueberries in medium bowl. Add sugar; toss to coat. Arrange berries over pie filling; refrigerate until ready to serve. Top with whipped cream, if desired.

Grasshopper Pie

Makes
8 servings

2 cups graham cracker crumbs

¼ cup unsweetened cocoa powder

¼ cup (½ stick) butter, melted

1 package (8 ounces) cream cheese, softened

¼ cup sugar

1 cup milk

1½ teaspoons vanilla

1 teaspoon mint extract

4 to 6 drops green food coloring (optional)

1 container (8 ounces) thawed frozen whipped topping

Chocolate curls (optional)

1 Spray 9-inch pie plate with nonstick cooking spray.

2 Combine graham cracker crumbs, cocoa and butter in medium bowl; mix well. Press onto bottom and up side of prepared pie plate. Refrigerate while preparing filling.

3 Beat cream cheese and sugar in large bowl with electric mixer at medium speed until fluffy. Gradually beat in milk until smooth. Stir in vanilla, mint extract and food coloring, if desired, until blended. Fold in whipped topping until blended. Refrigerate 20 minutes or until chilled but not set.

4 Pour filling into chilled crust. Freeze 4 hours or until set. Garnish with chocolate curls.

Chocolate Pie

Makes
8 servings

½ cup biscuit baking mix

1¼ cups sugar

3 tablespoons unsweetened cocoa powder, plus additional for garnish

3 egg whites

1 egg

2 tablespoons butter, melted

1½ teaspoons vanilla

Whipped cream and sliced fresh strawberries (optional)

1 Preheat oven to 350°F.

2 Spray 9-inch pie plate with nonstick cooking spray.

3 Combine baking mix, sugar and 3 tablespoons cocoa in large bowl; mix well. Add egg whites, egg, butter and vanilla; beat until smooth and well blended. Pour into prepared pie plate.

4 Bake 40 minutes or until toothpick inserted into center comes out clean. Serve with whipped cream and strawberries; sprinkle with additional cocoa, if desired.

Pear Almond Custard Pie

Makes
8 servings

1 can (28 ounces) pear halves in juice, drained, diced

2 cups whole milk

4 eggs

½ cup biscuit baking mix

½ cup sugar

¼ cup (½ stick) butter, melted and cooled

½ teaspoon almond extract

¼ teaspoon ground nutmeg

½ cup sliced almonds

1 Preheat oven to 350°F.

2 Spray 9-inch deep-dish glass pie plate with nonstick cooking spray.

3 Spread pears evenly in prepared pie plate. Combine milk, eggs, baking mix, sugar, butter, almond extract and nutmeg in large bowl; beat until well blended. Pour over pears. Sprinkle with almonds.

4 Bake 60 to 65 minutes or until knife inserted into center comes out clean. Cool completely on wire rack.

Speedy Double Strawberry Cream Pie

Makes
8 servings

4   ounces cream cheese, softened

3   tablespoons sugar

1   (6-ounce) graham cracker pie crust

⅓   cup seedless strawberry fruit spread

3   cups fresh strawberries, hulled and cut into ¼-inch slices

1   Beat cream cheese and sugar in medium bowl until smooth. Spread gently over bottom of crust.

2   Whisk fruit spread in small bowl until smooth. Spread 3 tablespoons fruit spread over cream cheese layer.

3   Place strawberries in large bowl. Add remaining fruit spread; toss gently to coat. Arrange strawberries over fruit spread layer. Refrigerate 1 hour or until chilled.

Favorite Peanut Butter Pie

Makes
8 servings

¾ cup creamy peanut butter, divided

1 (9-inch) shortbread cookie crumb pie crust

½ cup peanut butter chips, divided

1 package (3 ounces) cream cheese, softened

1 cup powdered sugar

1 container (8 ounces) thawed frozen whipped topping

1 Spread ¼ cup peanut butter over bottom of crust. Sprinkle with ¼ cup peanut butter chips.

2 Beat cream cheese and sugar in medium bowl with electric mixer at medium speed until creamy. Add remaining ½ cup peanut butter; beat until light and fluffy. Fold in whipped topping.

3 Pour into pie crust; sprinkle with remaining ¼ cup peanut butter chips. Serve immediately or refrigerate until ready to serve.

Buttermilk Pie

Makes
8 servings

1½ cups sugar

1 tablespoon cornstarch

3 eggs

½ cup buttermilk

¼ cup (½ stick) butter, melted and cooled

1 tablespoon lemon juice

1 teaspoon vanilla

1 (6-ounce) graham cracker pie crust

Whipped cream (optional)

1 Preheat oven to 350°F.

2 Combine sugar and cornstarch in medium bowl; mix well. Add eggs, buttermilk, butter, lemon juice and vanilla; beat with electric mixer at medium speed until smooth. Pour into crust.

3 Bake 40 minutes or until set. Cool completely on wire rack. Refrigerate 2 hours or until ready to serve. Serve with whipped cream, if desired.

Mocha Cappuccino Ice Cream Pie

Makes
8 servings

¼ cup cold water

1 tablespoon instant coffee granules

2½ tablespoons sugar

½ teaspoon vanilla

4 cups fudge marble ice cream, softened

1 (6-ounce) graham cracker pie crust

Whipped cream (optional)

1 Combine water, coffee granules, sugar and vanilla in small bowl; stir until coffee granules are dissolved.

2 Combine ice cream and coffee mixture in large bowl; stir gently until blended. Spread evenly in crust. Cover and freeze 4 hours or until firm.

3 Let stand at room temperature 10 minutes before serving. Top with whipped cream, if desired.

So-Easy Peach Pie

Makes
8 servings

1 refrigerated pie crust (half of 15-ounce package)

1 package (16 ounces) frozen sliced peaches, thawed, juice reserved

2 teaspoons cornstarch

½ cup golden raisins

4 tablespoons sugar, divided

1 teaspoon vanilla or almond extract

¼ teaspoon ground cinnamon (optional)

1 Let crust stand at room temperature 15 minutes. Preheat oven to 450°F.

2 Spray large baking sheet with nonstick cooking spray or line with parchment paper.

3 Unroll crust on prepared baking sheet. Roll or flute edge, if desired. Prick holes in crust several times with fork. Bake 10 to 12 minutes or until golden brown.

4 Combine peach juice and cornstarch in large nonstick skillet; stir until cornstarch is dissolved. Add peaches and raisins; bring to a boil over high heat. Boil 2 minutes, stirring occasionally. Remove from heat; stir in 3 tablespoons sugar, vanilla and cinnamon, if desired.

5 Slide baked crust over peach mixture in skillet. Sprinkle with remaining 1 tablespoon sugar.

Vanilla Pumpkin Pie

Makes
8 servings

1 package (4-serving size) vanilla instant pudding and
   pie filling mix

1½ cups milk

1 cup canned solid-pack pumpkin

¼ teaspoon ground cinnamon

¼ teaspoon ground nutmeg

1 teaspoon sugar

1 baked 9-inch pie crust

1 Beat pudding mix and milk in medium bowl until blended.
Add pumpkin, cinnamon, nutmeg and sugar; beat until
well blended.

2 Pour filling into baked crust. Refrigerate 3 hours or until firm.

★ Tip: This pie can be prepared a day in advance and refrigerated
    overnight.

Sour Cream Cranberry Pie

Makes
8 servings

2 eggs

2 egg yolks

1½ cups reduced-fat sour cream

1 cup granulated sugar

½ teaspoon vanilla

¼ teaspoon salt

1 cup dried cranberries

1 unbaked 9-inch pie crust

Powdered sugar (optional)

1 Preheat oven to 350°F.

2 Beat eggs and egg yolks in large bowl. Add sour cream, granulated sugar, vanilla and salt; beat until well blended. Stir in cranberries. Pour into unbaked crust. Place pie on baking sheet.

3 Bake 50 minutes or until set. Cool on wire rack. Refrigerate 4 hours or overnight. Sprinkle with powdered sugar just before serving, if desired.

★ Tip: Do not substitute full-fat or fat-free sour cream.

Black and White Pie

Makes
8 servings

2 cups chocolate cookie crumbs

6 tablespoons (¾ stick) butter, melted

7 tablespoons Irish cream liqueur, divided

½ (8-ounce) package cream cheese, softened

2 tablespoons milk

1 package (4-serving size) white chocolate instant pudding and pie filling mix

2 cups whipped topping

Chocolate Curls (recipe follows, optional)

1 Preheat oven to 350°F. Combine cookie crumbs, butter and 3 tablespoons liqueur in medium bowl; mix well. Press onto bottom and up side of 9-inch pie plate. Bake 3 minutes. Cool completely on wire rack.

2 Beat cream cheese, milk and remaining 4 tablespoons liqueur in large bowl until blended. Add pudding mix; beat until well blended. Stir in whipped topping. Pour into crust. Refrigerate 1 to 2 hours or until firm.

3 Prepare Chocolate Curls, if desired. Sprinkle over pie.

Chocolate Curls: Soften 2 (1-ounce) squares semisweet or milk chocolate by setting chocolate in warm place for 30 minutes. (Chocolate should still be firm.) Pull vegetable peeler across chocolate to create curls. Refrigerate curls on waxed paper-lined baking sheet about 15 minutes or until firm. Repeat for white chocolate curls, omitting softening step.

Celia's Flat Fruit Pie

Makes
12 servings

2 packages (8 ounces each) dried mixed fruit
  (pitted prunes, pears, apples, apricots and peaches)

3 cups water

½ cup sugar

½ teaspoon ground cinnamon

¼ teaspoon ground cloves

Flaky Pastry (recipe follows)

1 teaspoon lemon juice

1 Combine dried fruit, water, sugar, cinnamon and cloves in large saucepan; cook over medium heat until sugar is dissolved, stirring occasionally. Reduce heat to low; cover and simmer 45 minutes or until fruit is tender. Meanwhile, prepare Flaky Pastry.

2 Pour fruit mixture into blender or food processor; blend until fruit is coarsely puréed. (Purée should measure 3 cups. If purée measures more, return to saucepan and cook until reduced to 3 cups, stirring frequently.) Stir in lemon juice. Cool completely.

3 Preheat oven to 400°F. Roll out one disc of dough into 13-inch circle on floured surface. Place on 12-inch pizza pan, trimming to leave ½-inch overhang. Spread fruit purée over dough. Roll out remaining disc of dough into 13-inch circle; place over filling. Cut slits in center. Fold edge of top crust under edge of bottom crust; seal and flute.

4 Bake 35 minutes or until golden brown. Cool on wire rack 1 hour.

Flaky Pastry: Combine 3⅓ cups flour and ¾ teaspoon salt in medium bowl. Cut in 1 cup cold cubed shortening with pastry blender or two knives until mixture resembles coarse crumbs. Sprinkle with 6 to 8 tablespoons cold water, 1 tablespoon at a time, stirring until dough forms. Divide dough in half. Shape each half into a disc; wrap with plastic wrap. Refrigerate 30 minutes.

Pumpkin Pie with Honey-Glazed Pecans

Makes
6 to 8 servings

1 refrigerated pie crust (half of 15-ounce package)

2 eggs

1 can (15 ounces) solid-pack pumpkin

⅔ cup packed brown sugar

1 teaspoon ground cinnamon

¾ teaspoon ground ginger

½ teaspoon salt

¼ teaspoon ground nutmeg

¼ teaspoon ground allspice

1 can (12 ounces) evaporated milk

Honey-Glazed Pecans (recipe follows)

Whipped topping

1 Preheat oven to 425°F. Line 9-inch pie plate with crust; flute edge.

2 Beat eggs in large bowl. Add pumpkin, brown sugar, cinnamon, ginger, salt, nutmeg and allspice; beat until well blended. Stir in evaporated milk. Pour into crust.

3 Bake 15 minutes. *Reduce oven temperature to 350°F.* Bake 30 to 35 minutes or until center is set. Cool on wire rack. Refrigerate until ready to serve.

4 Meanwhile, prepare Honey-Glazed Pecans. Top pie with whipped cream and pecans.

Honey-Glazed Pecans: Combine 1 tablespoon honey, ¼ teaspoon ground cinnamon and ⅛ teaspoon salt in small bowl; mix well. Add ½ cup pecan halves; stir until pecans are completely coated. Spread pecans on parchment paper-lined baking sheet, making sure pecans do not touch. Bake in preheated 350°F oven about 15 minutes. Slide parchment paper onto counter; cool pecans before using.

Lemon-Lime Meringue Pie

Makes
8 servings

1 unbaked 9-inch deep-dish pie crust

4 eggs, separated

¾ cup plus 1 tablespoon sugar, divided

⅛ teaspoon salt

1 tablespoon cornstarch

½ cup whipping cream

3 tablespoons lemon juice

2 teaspoons grated lemon peel

3 tablespoons lime juice

2 teaspoons grated lime peel

2 tablespoons butter, cut into small pieces

1 Preheat oven to 400°F. Prick holes in bottom of unbaked crust with fork. Bake 10 minutes or until lightly browned. Cool completely on wire rack.

2 *Reduce oven temperature to 325°F.* Beat egg yolks, ½ cup plus 1 tablespoon sugar and salt in medium saucepan until blended. Stir cornstarch into cream in small bowl until smooth. Stir into egg yolk mixture.

3 Add lemon juice, lemon peel, lime juice and lime peel; cook and stir over medium heat until thickened. Remove from heat; stir in butter until melted. Pour into crust.

4 Beat egg whites in medium bowl with electric mixer at medium speed until frothy. Add remaining ¼ cup sugar, 1 tablespoon at a time, beating at high speed after each addition until stiff and glossy. Gently spread meringue over filling.

5 Bake 20 minutes or until meringue is golden brown. Cool completely on wire rack.

Upside-Down Apple Pie

Makes
8 servings

¼ cup (½ stick) butter, softened

½ cup pecan halves

½ cup packed brown sugar

1 package (about 15 ounces) refrigerated pie crusts (2 crusts)

4 large Granny Smith apples, peeled and cut into ¼-inch slices

4 teaspoons lemon juice

½ cup granulated sugar

1 tablespoon all-purpose flour

1 teaspoon ground cinnamon

¾ teaspoon ground nutmeg

1 Preheat oven to 400°F. Spread butter evenly on bottom and up side of 9-inch pie plate. Press pecans into butter, rounded sides down. Pat brown sugar evenly over pecans. Roll out one crust on lightly floured surface to fit pie plate; place over pecans. Trim edge even with edge of pie plate.

2 Combine apples and lemon juice in large bowl; toss to coat. Add granulated sugar, flour, cinnamon and nutmeg; toss to coat.

3 Place apple mixture in crust; spread evenly to make top level. Roll out remaining crust to fit over top of pie. Place crust over apple mixture; trim edge, leaving ½-inch overhang. Fold overhang under so crust is even with edge of pie plate. Crimp or flute edge. Pierce top crust with fork.

4 Bake 50 minutes. Cool on wire rack 5 minutes. Place serving plate over pie plate; invert pie onto serving plate. Serve warm or at room temperature.

Caribbean Coconut Pie

Makes
8 servings

1   unbaked 9-inch deep-dish pie crust

1   can (14 ounces) sweetened condensed milk

¾   cup flaked coconut

2   eggs

½   cup hot water

2   teaspoons grated lime peel

    Juice of 1 lime

¼   teaspoon salt

⅛   teaspoon ground red pepper

    Whipped cream (optional)

1   Preheat oven to 400°F.

2   Prick holes in bottom of unbaked crust with fork. Bake 10 minutes or until lightly browned. Cool 15 minutes on wire rack.

3   *Reduce oven temperature to 350°F.* Beat sweetened condensed milk, coconut, eggs, water, lime peel, lime juice, salt and red pepper in large bowl until well blended. Pour into crust.

4   Bake 30 minutes or until knife inserted into center comes out clean. Cool completely on wire rack. Top with whipped cream, if desired.

Lattice-Topped Deep-Dish Cherry Pie

Makes
9 servings

2   cans (about 14 ounces each) pitted tart red cherries in water

½   cup sugar

3   tablespoons quick-cooking tapioca

¼   teaspoon almond extract

¾   cup all-purpose flour

¼   teaspoon salt

3   tablespoons cold shortening, cut into small pieces

2   to 3 tablespoons cold water

1   Preheat oven to 375°F. Drain one can of cherries. Combine drained cherries, remaining can of cherries with juice, sugar, tapioca and almond extract in large bowl; mix well.

2   Combine flour and salt in medium bowl. Cut in shortening with pastry blender or two knives until mixture resembles coarse crumbs. Add water, 1 tablespoon at a time, stirring just until moistened. Shape dough into a ball.

3   Roll out dough into 9×8-inch rectangle on lightly floured surface. Cut into nine 8×1-inch strips.

4   Spoon cherry mixture into 13×9-inch baking dish. Place four dough strips diagonally over cherry mixture as shown in photo. Weave remaining five dough strips across diagonal strips to create lattice. Pinch strips at ends to seal.

5   Bake 40 to 50 minutes or until filling is bubbly and crust is golden brown. Cool slightly on wire rack.

Baked Alaska Apple Butter Pie

Makes
8 servings

Single Crust Pie Pastry (recipe follows)

2 cups apple butter

1 can (12 ounces) evaporated milk

3 egg yolks, beaten

¼ cup packed brown sugar

1 pint butter pecan ice cream, softened

Brown Sugar Meringue (recipe follows)

1 Preheat oven to 425°F. Prepare Single Crust Pie Pastry. Roll out dough into 11-inch circle on floured surface. Line 9-inch pie plate with dough; flute edge.

2 Beat apple butter, evaporated milk, egg yolks and ¼ cup brown sugar in medium bowl until well blended. Pour into crust.

3 Bake 15 minutes. *Reduce oven temperature to 350°F.* Bake 45 minutes or until knife inserted into center comes out clean. Cool completely on wire rack. Cover and refrigerate at least 1 hour or until ready to serve.

4 Meanwhile, line inside of 8-inch pie plate with plastic wrap. Spread ice cream in prepared pie plate. Cover and freeze until firm.

5 Just before serving, preheat oven to 500°F. Prepare Brown Sugar Meringue. Unmold ice cream and invert onto chilled pie. Spread meringue over ice cream and any exposed surface of pie, covering completely. Bake 2 to 3 minutes or until meringue is golden brown. Serve immediately.

Single Crust Pie Pastry: Combine 1¼ cups flour and ½ teaspoon salt in medium bowl. Cut in 3 tablespoons cold cubed shortening and 3 tablespoons cold cubed butter with pastry blender or two knives until mixture resembles coarse crumbs. Combine 3 tablespoons cold water and ½ teaspoon cider vinegar in small bowl. Add to flour mixture; mix with fork until dough forms, adding additional water as needed. Shape dough into a disc; wrap with plastic wrap. Refrigerate 30 minutes.

Brown Sugar Meringue: Beat 3 egg whites and ¼ teaspoon cream of tartar in small bowl with electric mixer at high speed until foamy. Beat in ½ teaspoon vanilla. Add 6 tablespoons packed brown sugar, 1 tablespoon at a time; beat until stiff peaks form.

Turtle Pecan Pie

Makes
8 servings

1 unbaked 9-inch deep-dish pie crust

1 cup light corn syrup

3 eggs, lightly beaten

½ cup sugar

⅓ cup butter, melted

1 teaspoon vanilla

½ teaspoon salt

1¼ cups pecans, toasted*

2 squares (1 ounce each) semisweet chocolate, melted

½ cup caramel ice cream topping

Whipped cream (optional)

Grated chocolate (optional)

To toast pecans, spread on baking sheet. Bake in preheated 350°F oven 5 to 7 minutes or until lightly browned.

1 Preheat oven to 350°F. Place unbaked crust on baking sheet.

2 Beat corn syrup, eggs, sugar, butter, vanilla and salt in large bowl until well blended. Reserve ½ cup egg mixture. Stir 1 cup pecans and chocolate into remaining egg mixture; pour into crust. Stir caramel topping into reserved egg mixture; carefully pour over pecan filling.

3 Bake 50 to 55 minutes or until filling is set about 3 inches from edge. Cool completely on wire rack. Top with whipped cream and grated chocolate, if desired.

Orange Plum and Apple Open-Faced Pie

Makes
8 servings

1 refrigerated pie crust (half of 15-ounce package)

4 cups sliced peeled Gala apples (about 4 medium)

10 orange essence dried plums,* finely chopped

1 teaspoon vanilla

½ teaspoon grated orange peel

2 tablespoons orange juice

1 tablespoon cornstarch

2 teaspoons granulated sugar

If orange essence plums are not available, use regular dried plums.

1 Preheat oven to 425°F.

2 Line large baking sheet with parchment paper or spray with nonstick cooking spray. Place pie crust on baking sheet.

3 Combine apples, dried plums, vanilla and orange peel in medium bowl; mix well. Stir orange juice into cornstarch in small bowl until cornstarch is dissolved. Add to apple mixture; toss to coat.

4 Spread apple mixture over crust, leaving 2-inch border around edge. Fold edge of crust up and over filling, overlapping as necessary. Press gently to secure crust to filling. Sprinkle crust with sugar.

5 Bake 30 to 35 minutes or until apples are tender and crust is golden brown.

Almond Custard Pie

Makes
8 servings

- 1½ cups all-purpose flour
- ½ cup plus 1 tablespoon granulated sugar, divided
- ½ teaspoon salt, divided
- ½ cup (1 stick) butter, melted
- 3 eggs
- ¼ teaspoon ground cinnamon
- 2 cups half-and-half
- ½ teaspoon almond extract
- 1 tablespoon butter
- ¾ cup sliced almonds
- 2 tablespoons packed dark brown sugar

1 Preheat oven to 425°F. Combine flour, 1 tablespoon granulated sugar and ¼ teaspoon salt in large bowl; mix well. Gradually add ½ cup melted butter, stirring until dough forms.

2 Place dough in 9-inch pie plate; press onto bottom and up side of pie plate, forming high rim. Place on baking sheet. Bake 5 minutes. (It is not necessary to weigh down crust.)

3 *Reduce oven temperature to 325°F.* Beat eggs in large bowl. Add remaining ½ cup granulated sugar, ¼ teaspoon salt and cinnamon; beat until well blended. Stir in half-and-half and almond extract.

4 Melt 1 tablespoon butter in medium skillet over medium heat. Add almonds; cook and stir 2 minutes or until golden brown. Remove from heat; cool slightly. Pour custard into crust. Spread almonds over custard; sprinkle with brown sugar.

5 Bake 30 minutes or until set. Cool on wire rack 30 minutes. Serve at room temperature or chilled.

Note: You can substitute an unbaked 9-inch deep-dish pie crust for the homemade crust, if desired. Let the crust stand at room temperature 15 minutes. Prick holes in the bottom of the crust with a fork. Bake 5 minutes as directed for the homemade crust.

Pie for Dinner

Talkin' Turkey Pot Pie

Makes
6 servings

2 tablespoons butter

1 medium onion, chopped

3 tablespoons all-purpose flour

½ teaspoon dried thyme

¼ teaspoon black pepper

1 can (about 14 ounces) chicken broth

1 package (16 ounces) frozen mixed vegetables

2 cups chopped cooked turkey

1 refrigerated pie crust (half of 15-ounce package)

1 egg, beaten

1 Preheat oven to 400°F. Melt butter in large saucepan over medium heat. Add onion; cook and stir 5 minutes or until tender. Add flour, thyme and pepper; cook and stir 1 minute. Add broth; bring to a boil.

2 Stir in vegetables and turkey. Reduce heat to medium-low; cook 5 minutes or until heated through. Pour into 9-inch deep-dish pie plate or 2-quart casserole. Top with crust; seal edge and flute. Brush crust with egg.

3 Bake 25 minutes or until crust is golden brown.

Steak and Mushroom Pie

Makes
4 to 6 servings

3 tablespoons butter, divided

1½ pounds boneless beef chuck steak, cut into 1-inch cubes

2 medium onions, chopped

3 stalks celery, cut into ½-inch slices

1 package (8 ounces) sliced mushrooms

½ teaspoon dried thyme

½ cup red wine

¼ cup all-purpose flour

1 cup reduced-sodium beef broth

2 tablespoons tomato paste

1 tablespoon Dijon mustard

½ teaspoon salt

¼ teaspoon black pepper

1 refrigerated pie crust (half of 15-ounce package)

1 egg, lightly beaten

1 Spray 9-inch deep-dish pie plate or 1½-quart baking dish with nonstick cooking spray. Melt 2 tablespoons butter in large saucepan over medium-high heat. Add half of beef; cook 5 minutes or until browned, turning occasionally. Remove to plate; repeat with remaining beef.

2 Melt remaining 1 tablespoon butter in same saucepan over medium-high heat. Add onions, celery, mushrooms and thyme; cook and stir 4 to 5 minutes or until vegetables begin to soften. Add wine; cook and stir 3 to 4 minutes or until almost evaporated. Add flour; cook and stir 1 minute. Stir in broth, tomato paste, mustard and beef; bring to a boil. Reduce heat to medium-low; cover and simmer 1 hour to 1 hour 10 minutes or until beef is very tender, stirring occasionally. Remove from heat; stir in salt and pepper. Pour into prepared pie plate; let cool 20 minutes.

3 Preheat oven to 400°F. Roll out crust on lightly floured surface to fit top of pie plate. Place crust over filling; flute or crimp edge. Brush crust with egg; cut several small slits in crust with tip of knife.

4 Bake 23 to 25 minutes or until crust is golden brown. Let stand 5 minutes before serving.

Impossibly Easy Salmon Pie

Makes
8 servings

1 can (7½ ounces) red salmon, drained and deboned
½ cup grated Parmesan cheese
¼ cup sliced green onions
1 jar (2 ounces) chopped pimientos, drained
½ cup cottage cheese
1 tablespoon lemon juice
1½ cups milk
3 eggs
¾ cup biscuit baking mix
½ teaspoon salt
¼ teaspoon dried dill weed
¼ teaspoon paprika (optional)

1 Preheat oven to 375°F. Spray 9-inch pie plate with nonstick cooking spray.

2 Combine salmon, Parmesan cheese, green onions and pimientos in prepared pie plate; mix well.

3 Combine cottage cheese and lemon juice in blender or food processor; blend until smooth. Add milk, eggs, baking mix, salt and dill weed; blend 15 seconds. Pour over salmon mixture. Sprinkle with paprika, if desired.

4 Bake 35 to 40 minutes or until golden brown and knife inserted near center comes out clean. Let stand 5 minutes before serving.

Lamb and Vegetable Pie

Makes
4 to 6 servings

2   tablespoons vegetable oil

1½ pounds boneless leg of lamb, cut into 1-inch cubes

3   medium russet potatoes (about 12 ounces), peeled and cut into 1-inch cubes

16 frozen pearl onions (about 1 cup)

1   cup frozen peas and carrots

3   tablespoons all-purpose flour

1½ cups reduced-sodium beef broth

3   tablespoons chopped fresh parsley

2   tablespoons tomato paste

2   teaspoons Worcestershire sauce

½   teaspoon salt

¼   teaspoon black pepper

1   refrigerated pie crust (half of 15-ounce package)

1   egg, lightly beaten

1 Spray 9-inch deep-dish baking dish or pie plate with nonstick cooking spray. Heat oil in large saucepan over medium-high heat. Add half of lamb; cook 4 to 5 minutes or until browned, turning occasionally. Remove lamb to plate; repeat with remaining lamb.

2 Add potatoes, onions and peas and carrots to saucepan; cook 2 minutes, stirring occasionally. Stir in lamb and any accumulated juices; cook 2 minutes. Add flour; cook and stir 1 minute. Stir in broth, parsley, tomato paste, Worcestershire sauce, salt and pepper; bring to a boil. Reduce heat to medium-low; cover and simmer about 30 minutes or until lamb and potatoes are tender, stirring occasionally. Pour into prepared baking dish; let cool 20 minutes.

3   Preheat oven to 400°F. Place crust over filling; flute or crimp edge.
    Brush crust with egg; cut several small slits in crust with tip of
    knife.

4   Bake about 25 minutes or until filling is thick and bubbly and crust
    is golden brown. Let stand 5 minutes before serving.

Country Chicken Pot Pie

Makes
6 servings

2 tablespoons butter

1 pound boneless skinless chicken breasts, cut into 1-inch pieces

¾ teaspoon salt

8 ounces fresh green beans, cut into 1-inch pieces (2 cups)

½ cup chopped red bell pepper

½ cup thinly sliced celery

3 tablespoons all-purpose flour

½ cup chicken broth

½ cup half-and-half

1 teaspoon dried thyme

½ teaspoon dried sage

1 cup frozen pearl onions

½ cup frozen corn

Pastry for single-crust 10-inch pie

1 Preheat oven to 425°F. Spray 10-inch deep-dish pie plate with nonstick cooking spray.

2 Melt butter in large deep skillet over medium-high heat. Add chicken; cook and stir 3 minutes or until no longer pink in center. Sprinkle with salt. Add beans, bell pepper and celery; cook and stir 3 minutes.

3 Add flour; cook and stir 1 minute. Stir in broth, half-and-half, thyme and sage; bring to a boil over high heat. Reduce heat to low; simmer 3 minutes or until thickened. Stir in onions and corn. Return to a simmer; cook and stir 1 minute. Pour into prepared pie plate.

4 Place crust over filling; turn edge under and flute or crimp edge. Cut several small slits in crust with tip of knife.

5 Bake 20 minutes or until filling is hot and bubbly and crust is golden brown. Let stand 5 minutes before serving.

Hometown Deep-Dish Vegetable Pie

Makes
6 servings

¼ cup (½ stick) plus 1 tablespoon butter, softened, divided

2 cups small broccoli florets (about ¾-inch pieces)

1½ cups sliced mushrooms (about 4 ounces)

1 cup chopped red bell pepper

¾ cup finely chopped green onions (about 1 bunch)

1¼ cups biscuit baking mix

1½ tablespoons water

1 cup (4 ounces) shredded Swiss cheese

½ cup (2 ounces) shredded sharp Cheddar cheese

1½ cups whole milk

3 large eggs

½ teaspoon salt

⅛ teaspoon ground red pepper

1 Preheat oven to 375°F. Spray 9-inch deep-dish pie plate with nonstick cooking spray.

2 Melt 1 tablespoon butter in medium nonstick skillet. Add broccoli, mushrooms and bell pepper; cover and cook 2 minutes, stirring occasionally. Remove from heat; stir in green onions.

3 Combine baking mix, remaining ¼ cup butter and water in small bowl; stir to form soft dough. Shape dough into a ball; flatten into disc. Press dough evenly onto bottom and up side of prepared pie plate. Pour vegetable mixture into crust; top with cheeses. Beat milk, eggs, salt and red pepper in medium bowl until well blended. Pour over vegetable mixture.

4 Bake 40 minutes or until center is set and knife inserted into center comes out clean. Let stand 15 minutes before serving.

Quick Turkey Pot Pie

Makes
5 servings

2 teaspoons olive oil

1 cup diced red bell pepper

2 stalks celery, sliced

1 small onion, chopped

¾ cup plus 2 tablespoons all-purpose flour, divided

1¼ cups chicken broth

1 cup cubed peeled potato

½ teaspoon dried thyme

¼ teaspoon plus ⅛ teaspoon salt, divided

¼ teaspoon black pepper

2 cups cubed cooked turkey breast (about 10 ounces)

⅓ cup frozen peas

¾ teaspoon baking powder

⅛ teaspoon baking soda

3 tablespoons cold butter, cut into small pieces

3 to 5 tablespoons buttermilk

1 Preheat oven to 425°F.

2 Heat oil in large skillet over medium heat. Add bell pepper, celery and onion; cook and stir 4 to 5 minutes. Stir in 2 tablespoons flour until blended. Stir in broth, potato, thyme, ¼ teaspoon salt and black pepper; bring to a boil. Reduce heat to low; cover and simmer 8 to 10 minutes. Stir in turkey and peas; simmer 5 to 7 minutes or until potato is tender and peas are hot. Pour into 1- to 1½-quart casserole.

3   Combine remaining ¾ cup flour, ⅛ teaspoon salt, baking powder
and baking soda in medium bowl; mix well. Cut in butter with
pastry blender or two knives until mixture resembles coarse
crumbs. Stir in buttermilk until dough forms. Place on floured
surface; knead lightly. Pat out dough to about ½-inch thickness.
Cut into five biscuits with 2- to 2½-inch biscuit cutter, rerolling
dough as needed. Arrange biscuits over filling.

4   Bake 12 to 14 minutes or until biscuits are lightly browned.

Cheesy Tuna Pie

Makes
6 servings

2   cups cooked rice

2   cans (6 ounces each) tuna, drained and flaked

1   cup mayonnaise

1   cup (4 ounces) shredded Cheddar cheese

½   cup sour cream

½   cup thinly sliced celery

1   can (4 ounces) sliced black olives

2   tablespoons dried minced onion

1   refrigerated pie crust (half of 15-ounce package)

1   Preheat oven to 350°F.

2   Spray 9-inch deep-dish pie plate with nonstick cooking spray.

3   Combine rice, tuna, mayonnaise, cheese, sour cream, celery, olives and minced onion in medium bowl; mix well. Pour into prepared pie plate. Place crust over filling; press edge of crust into pie plate to seal. Cut several small slits in crust with tip of knife.

4   Bake 20 minutes or until filling is bubbly and crust is lightly browned.

Metric Conversion Chart

VOLUME MEASUREMENTS (dry)

$^1/_8$ teaspoon = 0.5 mL
$^1/_4$ teaspoon = 1 mL
$^1/_2$ teaspoon = 2 mL
$^3/_4$ teaspoon = 4 mL
1 teaspoon = 5 mL
1 tablespoon = 15 mL
2 tablespoons = 30 mL
$^1/_4$ cup = 60 mL
$^1/_3$ cup = 75 mL
$^1/_2$ cup = 125 mL
$^2/_3$ cup = 150 mL
$^3/_4$ cup = 175 mL
1 cup = 250 mL
2 cups = 1 pint = 500 mL
3 cups = 750 mL
4 cups = 1 quart = 1 L

VOLUME MEASUREMENTS (fluid)

1 fluid ounce (2 tablespoons) = 30 mL
4 fluid ounces ($^1/_2$ cup) = 125 mL
8 fluid ounces (1 cup) = 250 mL
12 fluid ounces (1$^1/_2$ cups) = 375 mL
16 fluid ounces (2 cups) = 500 mL

WEIGHTS (mass)

$^1/_2$ ounce = 15 g
1 ounce = 30 g
3 ounces = 90 g
4 ounces = 120 g
8 ounces = 225 g
10 ounces = 285 g
12 ounces = 360 g
16 ounces = 1 pound = 450 g

DIMENSIONS

$^1/_{16}$ inch = 2 mm
$^1/_8$ inch = 3 mm
$^1/_4$ inch = 6 mm
$^1/_2$ inch = 1.5 cm
$^3/_4$ inch = 2 cm
1 inch = 2.5 cm

OVEN TEMPERATURES

250°F = 120°C
275°F = 140°C
300°F = 150°C
325°F = 160°C
350°F = 180°C
375°F = 190°C
400°F = 200°C
425°F = 220°C
450°F = 230°C

BAKING PAN SIZES

Utensil	Size in Inches/Quarts	Metric Volume	Size in Centimeters
Baking or Cake Pan (square or rectangular)	8×8×2	2 L	20×20×5
	9×9×2	2.5 L	23×23×5
	12×8×2	3 L	30×20×5
	13×9×2	3.5 L	33×23×5
Loaf Pan	8×4×3	1.5 L	20×10×7
	9×5×3	2 L	23×13×7
Round Layer Cake Pan	8×1½	1.2 L	20×4
	9×1½	1.5 L	23×4
Pie Plate	8×1¼	750 mL	20×3
	9×1¼	1 L	23×3
Baking Dish or Casserole	1 quart	1 L	—
	1½ quart	1.5 L	—
	2 quart	2 L	—